ROMAN LAW IN CONTEXT

Roman Law in Context explains how Roman law worked for those who lived by it, by viewing it in the light of the society and economy in which it operated. The book discusses three main areas of Roman law and life: the family and inheritance; property and the use of land; commercial transactions and the management of businesses. It also deals with the question of litigation and how readily the Roman citizen could assert his or her legal rights in practice. In addition it provides an introduction to using the main sources of Roman law. The book ends with an epilogue discussing the role of Roman law in medieval and modern Europe, a bibliographical essay, and a glossary of legal terms. The book involves the minimum of legal technicality and is intended to be accessible to students and teachers of Roman history as well as interested general readers.

DAVID JOHNSTON is an advocate at the Scottish Bar and was Regius Professor of Civil Law in the University of Cambridge, and Fellow of Christ's College, from 1993 to 1999. His publications include: *On a Singular Book of Cervidius Scaevola* (1987), *The Roman Law of Trusts* (1988) and *Prescription and Limitation* (1999).

KEY THEMES IN ANCIENT HISTORY

Edited by P. A. CARTLEDGE *Clare College, Cambridge* and
P. D. A. GARNSEY *Jesus College, Cambridge*

Key Themes in Ancient History aims to provide readable, informed and original studies of various basic topics, designed in the first instance for students and teachers of Classics and Ancient History, but also for those engaged in related disciplines. Each volume is devoted to a general theme in Greek, Roman, or where appropriate, Graeco-Roman history, or to some salient aspect or aspects of it. Besides indicating the state of current research in the relevant area, authors seek to show how the theme is significant for our own as well as ancient culture and society. By providing books for courses that are oriented around themes it is hoped to encourage and stimulate promising new developments in teaching and research in ancient history.

Other books in the series

Death-ritual and social structure in classical antiquity, by Ian Morris
0 521 37465 0 (hardback), 0 521 37611 4 (paperback)

Literacy and orality in ancient Greece, by Rosalind Thomas
0 521 37346 8 (hardback), 0 521 37742 0 (paperback)

Slavery and society at Rome, by Keith Bradley
0 521 37287 9 (hardback), 0 521 37887 7 (paperback)

Law, violence, and community in classical Athens, by David Cohen
0 521 38167 3 (hardback), 0 521 38837 6 (paperback)

Public order in ancient Rome, by Wilfried Nippel
0 521 38327 7 (hardback), 0 521 38749 3 (paperback)

Friendship in the classical world, by David Konstan
0 521 45402 6 (hardback), 0 521 45998 2 (paperback)

Sport and society in ancient Greece, by Mark Golden
0 521 49698 5 (hardback), 0 521 49790 6 (paperback)

Food and society in classical antiquity, by Peter Garnsey
0 521 64182 9 (hardback), 0 521 64588 3 (paperback)

Religions of the ancient Greeks, by Simon Price
0 521 38201 7 (hardback), 0 521 38867 8 (paperback)

Banking and business in the Roman world, by Jean Andreau
0 521 38031 6 (hardback), 0 521 38932 1 (paperback)

ROMAN LAW IN CONTEXT

DAVID JOHNSTON

CAMBRIDGE
UNIVERSITY PRESS

CAMBRIDGE UNIVERSITY PRESS
Cambridge, New York, Melbourne, Madrid, Cape Town, Singapore, São Paulo, Delhi

Cambridge University Press
The Edinburgh Building, Cambridge CB2 8RU, UK

Published in the United States of America by Cambridge University Press, New York

www.cambridge.org
Information on this title: www.cambridge.org/9780521639613

First published 1999
Sixth printing 2008

Printed in the United Kingdom at the University Press, Cambridge

A catalogue record for this publication is available from the British Library

Library of Congress Cataloguing in Publication data
Johnston, David, 1961–
Roman law in context / David Johnston.
p. cm. (Key themes in ancient history)
Includes bibliographical references and index.
ISBN 0 521 63046 0 (hardback). ISBN 0 521 63961 1 (paperback)
1. Roman law – Popular works. 2. Justice, Administration of (Roman
law) – Popular works. 3. Rome – Social life and customs. 4. Rome –
Commerce. 1. Title. 11. Series.
KJA147.J64 1999
340.5′4–dc21 98-53582 CIP

ISBN 978-0-521-63046-7 hardback
ISBN 978-0-521-63961-3 paperback

For my parents

Contents

Preface

This book attempts to look at Roman law in its social and economic context. To do so is to court criticism from both historians and lawyers. The attempt, though arduous, is not quite doomed to failure: just over thirty years ago John Crook's deservedly successful *Law and Life of Rome* (1967) appealed to both camps. What need is there for anything more? Two points arise. First, if *Law and Life of Rome* aimed to illustrate the social and economic life of Rome through its law, the concern of the present book is more to understand the law in the light of the society and its economy.

Second, in the last thirty years there have been extraordinary finds of new evidence, especially inscriptions, and there have been remarkable developments in Roman social and economic history. A book which took proper account of all of this would be a good one. Unfortunately, this is not that book. To reflect all the new material would require a much longer treatment, and many years of painstaking composition.

This book therefore presents only a sketch, which may perhaps conjure up a faint image of what would be possible if the final work itself were ever to be executed. The book is aimed at historians rather than lawyers, and the choice of topics, emphasis in discussion, and bibliographical references all reflect that. The topic of commercial law is discussed more fully than the rest, partly because of its intrinsic interest and partly because it (unlike family law) has apparently not yet been much absorbed into the consciousness of historians.

For many constructive comments and suggestions I am most grateful to Peter Garnsey and Paul Cartledge, the editors of the series in which this book appears. The book would never have been finished had I not been able to enjoy the oasis of tranquillity that is the Robbins Collection at the Law School in Berkeley. For their hospitality and help I am glad to be able here to thank its staff and particularly its director, Laurent Mayali.

October 1998

CHAPTER I

Introduction

I WHAT IS NOT IN THIS BOOK

To begin with what is not in this book may seem odd; but it will otherwise remain unknown until the end, which seems unsatisfactory. This is not a comprehensive account of Roman law, or even of Roman law in its social setting. It is highly selective. There is nothing here about criminal law, and next to nothing about public or constitutional law. The focus is on the so-called classical period of Roman law, from about the end of the Roman republic in 31 BC until the death of the emperor Severus Alexander in AD 235. There is nothing here about post-classical law; and there is almost nothing about pre-classical law.

The warning about non-comprehensiveness is seriously intended. Law does not consist in generalities, and it is often said that the devil is in the detail. Undoubtedly that is right. But for present purposes it has been necessary to focus only on details which seem germane to the exploration at hand, of law and society. Many other details are glossed over, so anyone wanting a full account of the rules must look at one of the textbooks on the law. They are cited in the bibliographical essay at the end.

This chapter gives a rapid outline of the sources of Roman law, essentially for the purpose of making the ensuing discussion of substantive law comprehensible (fuller discussion may be found in Jolowicz and Nicholas 1972: 86–101, 353–94). The expression 'sources of Roman law' can mean two things: in the first sense it refers to where the law came from, statute, custom, decisions of courts and so forth; in the second it refers to how we know what we know about Roman law, our literary or documentary evidence of the past. The first of these senses is dealt with in this chapter; the second in the next. This chapter also deals briefly with the question how far the law at Rome was also the law in the provinces of the Roman empire.

II SOURCES OF LAW

From 509 BC the system of Roman government was republican. The popular assemblies elected magistrates, who held office for a year. The leading magistrates were the consuls, of whom there were two at a time, allegedly to prevent autocracy; next after them in the hierarchy were the praetors; and below them a range of other lesser magistrates. A senate of magistrates and former magistrates was the oligarchical element in the constitution, which advised the magistrates, and forwarded proposals for legislation to the popular assemblies.

1. The Twelve Tables

What we know of Roman private law begins in about 450 BC with the promulgation of the Twelve Tables. Livy and Cicero describe them as the source of all public and private law (Liv., *ab urbe condita* 3.34.6; Cic., *de oratore* 1.195); Cicero recounts how schoolchildren had to learn them (*de legibus* 2.59). What these Twelve Tables contained was not quite a law code in the modern sense but a list of important legal rules. The rules were extraordinarily laconic and nowadays are hard to understand, not least since the subject of successive clauses changes without warning. An example: 'If he summons him to law let him go; if he does not go, let him call witness; then let him take him' (1.1).

Since the Twelve Tables do not survive, our knowledge of them is extremely fragmentary, and the order in which provisions appeared in them is mostly not known. The provisions which are known indicate that matters of family law, property and succession were prominent, as is perhaps to be expected at this period, but they also attest great concern with setting out the rules for legal process.

2. Ius

Apart from the Twelve Tables, the early law of Rome consisted in customary or common law, which had not been created by enactment but was simply recognized as being the law. Some of this, of course, was what was ultimately embodied in the Twelve Tables. This old, unwritten, undeclared law was known as *ius*.

3. Statutes

Statutes were passed by the popular assemblies voting on proposals put before them by magistrates. Ancient authors liked to complain about the volume of legislation (Cic., *pro Balbo* 21; Liv., 3.34; Suetonius, *Iulius* 44.2; Tacitus, *Annals* 3.25). But so far as the private law was concerned, very little was made by statute (*lex*). There are notable exceptions, such as the statute on damage to property, the *lex Aquilia* of about 286 BC, and the *lex Falcidia* of 40 BC, which placed restrictions on legacies. But they are exceptions to a clear rule.

Statutes tended to be drafted in a very narrow and literal manner. Presumably this reflected extremely rigid canons of construction. An egregious example is provided by the *lex Rubria* dating from the 40s BC. Here, after setting out a model formula for trying an action which used the stock names 'Q. Licinius' and 'L. Seius' and the place name 'Mutina', the statute goes on to provide that the magistrate 'shall ensure that the names written in any of the foregoing formulae, and the name "Mutina" shall not be included or adopted in the said action, unless the said names written in any of the foregoing formulae shall belong to the persons who shall be parties to the said action, and unless the said matter shall be dealt with at Mutina . . .'.

None the less, there are clear signs of much bolder construction in other contexts: for example, the *lex Aquilia*, a much more concise statute (whose precise text is not preserved) gave damages for various wrongs including the breaking (*rumpere*) of a thing. Even in the later republic this statute was interpreted rather adventurously: *rumpere* came to be interpreted as damaging or impairing a thing in any way (*corrumpere*), and this interpretation greatly extended the scope of the statute (Ulpian, *D.* 9.2.27.13–35). But neither statutes nor statutory interpretation were characteristic of the development of Roman private law.

4. Praetor and edict

The formal source of most of Roman private law was the edict of the urban praetor, an office created in 367 BC which in the hierarchy ranked second only to the consuls. The praetor was the magistrate charged with the administration of justice. At the beginning of his year of office each praetor would publish in the forum his edict, which set out the legal remedies he would grant, together with the formulae for those remedies. How this system worked in litigation is discussed in chapter 6. A person who wished to raise legal proceedings would come before the praetor and request a particular formula from the edict. Equally, if he had a case which was not covered by an existing remedy in the edict, he might try to persuade the praetor to add a new remedy to the edict. In both the drafting of the initial edict and in its supplementation by new remedies the praetor, who would only rarely have knowledge about the law, would be assisted by the advice of legal experts, jurists. Behind the scenes, it was they who shaped the development of the praetor's edict.

Through his responsibility for granting legal remedies the praetor exercised control over the development of new causes of action. He could also lead to the suppression of old causes of action by refusing to grant remedies based on them, or by developing new defences available against them. The important point is that formally the praetor was not making new (substantive) law, a power which he as an individual magistrate did not have; all he was doing was creating new remedies or eroding old ones, exercising a procedural power. Indirectly, of course, the grant of a remedy in a new case was tantamount to the recognition of a new right; and the denial of an old remedy to the abolition of the right on which it was based. The Romans adhered to the theory that the praetor had no law-making power, but the jurists still referred to these new remedies as *ius honorarium*, 'law made in office', to be contrasted with *ius civile* (the law of the Twelve Tables, custom, and statute). While *ius civile*, which of course the praetor administered at the same time, theoretically ranked higher, in practice it was superseded where the *ius honorarium* took a different path.

The edict was a flexible instrument for reforming and modernizing the law, since changes could be made every year; and rejected again if need be. The greatest activity on the part of the praetors and the heyday of the edict as a source of law appear to have been in the second and first centuries BC. In practice much of the material must have continued unchanged from year to year; stability in the administration of justice required no less. Under the emperor Hadrian the jurist Julian was commissioned to draw up a finalized version of the edict; apparently he added only one clause (Marcellus, *D.* 37.8.3). It would be wrong to suppose that this was a strike by the emperor against the praetor's freedom to make new law; all the evidence suggests that edictal innovation had long since slowed to a trickle.

5. Jurists

There grew up a professional class of lawyers. These 'jurists' were originally priests, but in the course of the third century BC they came to
profess a secular jurisprudence. Their role in the Roman legal system
was pivotal: neither the magistrates responsible for granting legal remedies nor the judges who decided cases were lawyers; all looked to the
jurists for legal advice. Although the jurists did not in the modern sense
practise law, this contact with practice shaped their distinctly pragmatic
approach to it. But in debate and in their writing, they also developed a
sophisticated analytical jurisprudence; and particularly during the 'classical' period of Roman law – from the late republic until the early third
century AD – they produced a substantial legal literature. Typical of their
works were large-scale commentaries on civil law and the remedies contained in the magistrate's edict, and books of collected legal opinions.
While some of their works played their part in argument of interest only
to the jurists themselves, others were suited to, and written to satisfy, the
diverse demands of practice or even teaching.

During the early and high classical period, jurists seem to have
adhered to one of two schools, the Proculians and Sabinians. In precisely
what sense these were schools (of thought, of education) has been much
debated; and many have been the attempts to pin them down to
divergent political, philosophical or ideological positions. One point,
however, is perfectly clear: the two schools differed on a number of quite
fundamental legal principles and doctrines (Stein 1972; Liebs 1976;
Falchi 1981). Here are two examples:

(1) Oxen and horses and other beasts of draught and burden were *res
mancipi*, a type of property which required formal conveyance. The
schools differed on whether an animal became a *res mancipi* at birth or
only when it was actually capable of drawing or bearing burdens. In
abstract terms this amounts to a difference over the question whether it
is legitimate to describe something in a particular way on purely nominal
grounds or whether it must be capable of functioning in the terms
described (Gaius, *Inst.* 2.15).

(2) They differed on whether a new product (such as wine) made from
someone else's materials (grapes) belonged to the maker or to the owner
of the original materials. It is possible that this difference was founded
on philosophical reasoning about the identity of matter (Gaius, *Inst.*
2.79).

Although doctrinal disputes are commonplace in any legal system, it is difficult completely to suppress the feeling that some of these disputes were tainted by the luxury of self-indulgence and at the same time undermined legal certainty.

It is invidious to single out names, but space allows no alternative. Of the early classical jurists, leading figures were Proculus, Labeo, Sabinus. In the high classical period the leading figure is clearly Julian, head of the Sabinian school and author of a work entitled 'Digest' (*digesta*) in ninety books. His principal rival was Celsus, head of the Proculian school. Other notable jurists of the high-classical period were Neratius, Marcellus, Pomponius, Iavolenus and Scaevola. Gaius, the author of the Institutes, an elementary textbook, is in a peculiar position: unlike other leading jurists, he is not known to have held any political office and, in spite of his evident attachment to Sabinian views, there is little reason to associate him with Rome. But he is spoken of warmly by Justinian (*Gaius noster*), and it may well be that later law paid more attention to him than did his contemporaries.

In the late classical period the names of Papinian, Ulpian and Paul stand out: Papinian, author in particular of books of legal problems (*quaestiones*) and opinions (*responsa*) was regarded as the finest of the jurists. Under the system of ranking legal authorities devised in the fifth century his views were given exceptional weight. Ulpian and Paul were authors, among other things, of extensive commentaries on the praetor's edict (eighty-one and seventy-eight books *ad edictum*, respectively) and on the civil law in general (fifty-one and sixteen books *ad Sabinum*, respectively).

To give a sense of the range and style of juristic work is difficult in a short space; the excerpts from their works which appear in the following chapters may help. Here it must be sufficient to give just three examples. What emerges quite clearly from this is that the jurists were highly individual in style and in manner; this makes it all the more surprising that last century they were regarded as interchangeable or 'fungible'. That view has fortunately faded into history. Here are three opinions, *responsa*, very different in style.

Domitius Labeo to Celsus, greetings. I ask whether a person who is asked to write a will, and who not only wrote it but also signed it, can be regarded as one of the witnesses to it. Iuventius Celsus to Labeo, greeting. Either I do not understand your question or it is exceptionally stupid: it is quite absurd to doubt whether someone is a lawful witness because he also wrote the will himself. (Celsus, *D.* 28.1.27)

'I wish the income from the Aebutian farm to be given to my wife as long as she lives': I ask whether the heir's tutor can sell the farm and offer the legatee an annual payment of the rental income which the testator used to derive from the farm. He replied that he could. I also ask whether she can without penalty be prevented from living there. He replied that the heir was not obliged to provide accommodation. I also ask whether the heir is obliged to maintain the farm. He replied that, if the heir's actions cause a reduction in the income from the farm, the legatee can reasonably claim for that reduction in income. I also ask what the difference is between this legacy and a usufruct. He replied that the previous answers made the difference plain. (Scaevola, *D.* 33.2.38)

After a better offer has been made by a second buyer, the first buyer cannot sue him to recover money which he paid to the seller in advance against the price, unless there has been delegation by means of a promise. (Papinian, *D.* 18.2.20)

These opinions give a sense of the different characters and styles of the jurists. They also demonstrate the self-consciousness with which such opinions are given: Celsus bridles at being asked a stupid question; Scaevola comes close to doing the same. But what the opinions do have in common is an oracular style. Opinions are exactly that: opinions, and they rest on the prestige of the jurist. On that account the jurists can be brief, extremely brief, and they feel no need to give detailed reasons if any at all. Often the recital of the facts takes up most of the text; and the jurists confine themselves to giving an opinion 'on those facts' (*secundum ea quae proponerentur* is a frequent refrain). But they never express an opinion on whether the facts are correct, and they avoid answering factual questions: 'This is not a legal question.' Opinions in one or two words are far from uncommon; even 'why not?' is still an opinion, because it rests on the jurist's authority (Scaevola, *D.* 33.7.20.9; *D.* 34.1.19).

In the ancient world this self-conscious, perhaps arrogant, cultivation of authoritative knowledge about the law was peculiar to Roman legal culture. But legal culture was not, of course, impervious to outside influence. It is clear that in roughly the last century of the republic the jurists were particularly receptive to Greek influence, philosophical and rhetorical. Equally, from the late republic there was also mediation of Greek thought through the philosophical and rhetorical works of Cicero. Characteristic of this influence was a new (if short-lived) concern for system: Cicero is known to have contemplated writing (indeed perhaps he wrote) a work reducing the civil law to an art (*de iure civili in artem redigendo*); while the influence of dialectic is evident in the work of some late republican jurists. Some ideas found in the jurists can be traced back to Greek influence. On the extent of that influence a lively debate continues (Wieacker 1988: 618–62). However great it was, it is undeniable that the concerns of the Roman jurists were not philosophical: such material as they absorbed was turned to their own purposes, and was necessarily tempered with grosser unphilosophical considerations about reaching a workable result.

It was not only during the republic that the jurists were the key figures behind the scenes in the development of the law. Under the principate, the popular assemblies ceased to meet to pass statutes; in about AD 125 the praetor's edict was frozen in the form which it had then reached. Law which had previously been made by these means was now made by the emperor. But emperors were not lawyers. They too depended on the jurists for advice; and some of the leading jurists served in the imperial administration. Both Papinian and Ulpian had the distinction of holding the highest office of praetorian prefect. And the additional distinction of being murdered in office.

6. Emperor

The general term for law made by the emperor is 'constitution' (*constitutio*). This took many forms: if the ruling was made in court, it was known as a decree (*decretum*). Some emperors, such as Claudius and Septimius Severus were apparently fond of hearing court cases themselves (Suetonius, *Claud.* 14–15; Wolf 1994). Here is one of Paul's collection of *decreta* pronounced by Severus, which also gives a sense of the legal debate that might surround the emperor's decision:

Clodius Clodianus made a will and then in a second, invalid, will appointed the same heir: the heir wanted to accept the estate under the second will, since he thought it was valid, but then it was discovered not to be. Papinian thought he had repudiated the estate under the first will, and could not accept it under the second. I said he had not repudiated, since he thought the second will was valid. He [Severus] pronounced that Clodianus had died intestate. (Paul, *D.* 29.2.97)

Emperors might also issue general orders, known as edicts (*edicta*). Or they might reply to official inquiry by letter (*epistula*); or to inquiries made by private petitions, by writing the answer at the bottom of the petition: hence the name 'subscription' given to these replies. (In the third century 'rescript' comes to be the term applied to replies both to petitions and to letters.) Justinian's Code contains constitutions of all these sorts.

The surviving material makes it clear that the volume of material was massive. Two points follow. First, as would be expected, the emperor rarely initiated contact; mostly he merely responded to questions (Millar

1977). Second, the emperor had assistance. He had an office for answering letters and another for petitions; officials known as the secretaries *ab epistulis* and *a libellis* ran those offices, in which other staff worked. It seems likely that run of the mill inquiries would have been dealt with at a low level. The rescripts which survive in the Codes, which on the whole will have raised more difficult and interesting questions, were probably dealt with by the secretary *a libellis* personally, and from time to time the emperor is likely also to have been involved (Honoré 1994: 1–56).

Whenever a constitution required legal advice, it is the jurists who will have supplied it. It seems that under the empire a new class of civil-servant-jurists grew up. But in addition, as already mentioned, the great offices of state were sometimes held by leading jurists, and some (notably Papinian) are known to have held office as secretary *a libellis*.

III ROME AND THE PROVINCES

In the two and a half centuries of the classical period of Roman law the boundaries of the empire expanded. It covered a vast area, from Asia to Britain. Did the same law apply across this expanse, or was Roman law the law of Rome alone?

This is a difficult question, and a categorical answer to it would be ill-advised. Indeed, even to mention it is perhaps incautious. There must have been local and regional differences in the extent of Romanization. But the following points suggest that, in some areas at least, there were substantial similarities between Roman and provincial practice.

Governors of provinces were responsible for the administration of justice in their provinces, just as the praetors were in Rome. In just the same way they issued edicts. From the republic we have reasonable information about this, since one of Cicero's charges in his speeches against Verres is that he abused his position as governor by tampering with his edict (Cic., II *in Verrem* 1.119–21). That charge itself, while likely to be rhetorically exaggerated, does perhaps hint at an expectation that the provincial edict would remain fairly stable. Indeed, the administration of justice more or less requires that. In the second century AD Gaius wrote a commentary on the provincial edict, and it seems likely therefore that its text had been settled by then, just as had that of the urban edict about AD 125. It seems probable that the governor's edict in essentials mirrored the edict promulgated in Rome by the praetor.

It remains a matter of dispute whether the formulary system of Roman civil procedure (discussed in chapter 6) was applied throughout the provinces or was essentially confined to those classified as public provinces. The present concern, however, is with the question of Romanization, and it can be said with confidence that Roman legal practices were widely diffused through the provinces. Formulae which are faithful to the practice attested by juristic writings for Rome have been found in the Babatha archive in the province of Arabia, and in Transylvania, as well as in Spain and in the south of Italy (Wolff 1980; Kaser 1996: 163–71).

The Flavian municipal laws, of which substantial remnants survive for various Spanish municipalities, make very frequent reference to Roman practice, and indicate that the same procedures are to be followed in the municipality as in Rome. It is probable, however, that these represent an extreme of Romanization, so to treat them as representative of the rest of the empire would be unwise.

The extent of Romanization in these laws is particularly clear in the recently discovered *lex Irnitana*, a municipal statute originally set out on ten bronze tablets, from a town in Spain so small that it had never previously been heard of. Several chapters contain references to Roman practices for such things as which cases should be heard by single judges and which by several judges (*recuperatores*), and what time limits applied for hearing cases and for adjourning them (*lex Irn.* chs. K=49, 89, 91).

The most striking chapter of all is chapter 93, which provides 'For matters for which it is not expressly written or provided in this statute what law the citizens of the municipality of Irni should use among themselves, for all those matters let them use the civil law which Roman citizens use and shall use among themselves . . .'.

This is very remarkable. The provisions of Roman law were not merely displayed, laboriously engraved in bronze, but intended to be applied. The same picture is confirmed by two more chapters of the *lex Irnitana*: the first is concerned with setting the limits on the jurisdiction exercisable by the local magistrates at Irni and contains a long list of matters reserved to the higher authority of the provincial governor. What is interesting here is that for a wide range of legal actions it was actually the provincial governor who had jurisdiction: this will have served to reinforce the consistency with which Roman law was applied even in outlying parts of the empire. It is likely that the same would apply to outlying parts of Italy, except that there the higher jurisdiction would be that of the praetor (*lex Irn.* ch. 84).

The second of these chapters provides that the local magistrates are to display and to exercise their jurisdiction in accordance with the 'interdicts, edicts, formulae, promises (*sponsiones* and *stipulationes*), securities (*satis dationes*), defences, and prescriptions' set out in the edict of the provincial governor (*lex Irn.* ch. 85). Accordingly, even where the local jurisdiction was itself competent for the matter at issue, the local statute required that the citizens and residents of Irni should make use of Roman law as promulgated in the Roman governor's edict.

It cannot be said that the entire Roman empire was run on the footing of Spanish municipalities such as Irni, so it would not be legitimate to conclude that Romanization of this degree was universal. None the less, the formulae from the Babatha archive show that even in Arabia Roman law was being applied: in AD 124–5 Babatha, who was apparently not a Roman citizen, sued in the court of the Roman governor at Petra, where Roman law was applied. But this seems to have been a voluntary decision on her part; apparently the Jewish population made use of foreign laws and practices as well as their own. In short, within the empire there were local variations, places such as Arabia and Egypt where 'indigenous' legal orders survived and were happily tolerated by the Roman administration (Nörr 1998: 98; Cotton 1993: 101, 107; Modrzejewski 1970: 317–47; Kaser 1996: 167–8).

The evidence therefore supports a remarkable penetration of Roman legal culture wide throughout the empire. The grant of citizenship to virtually the whole population of the empire in AD 212 will have consolidated this process. But the role of Roman law in the provinces was not uniform, and our picture of it necessarily remains an impressionistic one.

CHAPTER 2

Sources and methodology

Chapter 1 dealt with the main sources of Roman private law, in the sense of the formal sources which created it. This chapter is concerned with the use of Roman legal sources by the modern student or scholar. It gives an account of those sources and problems that arise in using them. Nearly all the surviving material of Roman law is transmitted in one or other of the emperor Justinian's compilations. The chapter begins with an account of the sources which survive independently of Justinian; it then moves on to the Digest and (very briefly) other parts of the Justinianic compilations. It concludes with a general discussion of the difficulties of trying to write history based on legal sources.

The emphasis throughout is on questions peculiar to the legal sources. No detail, for example, is given about problems relating to the transmission of texts, since this is not specifically a problem of the legal sources but one which affects all ancient literature.

I SOURCES INDEPENDENT OF JUSTINIAN

1. Legal writings

The most important of the works which survive independently of the Justinianic compilations is the Institutes of Gaius, an elementary introduction to Roman law dating from about AD 160, and still the best introduction to the subject ever written. It contains a clear account of classical law and procedure, and also some valuable historical material of which the Digest preserves no record. It is preserved in a palimpsest discovered in Verona in 1816. It raises essentially the same textual critical problems as any other ancient work, and nothing in particular turns on the fact that it is a work about law.

A number of diverse legal productions survive of which only a few can be mentioned here:

(1) *Pauli sententiae*, 'the opinions of Paul', is a short account of Roman private law. Although attributed to Paul, it appears to date from the late third century AD and to derive from Africa (Liebs 1993: 32–43).

(2) Two works related to the Institutes of Gaius survive: (i) an epitome of the Institutes, which appears to date from the late fifth century (Liebs 1987: 175) and (ii) fragments known as the Autun Gaius, dating from the late third or early fourth century AD (Liebs 1987: 150). Both of these are western in origin.

(3) A short compendium ascribed to Ulpian, and sometimes known as the Epitome of Ulpian, survives, dating from about AD 320.

(4) The *Fragmenta Vaticana*, so-called because they are preserved in a Vatican manuscript, consist of lengthy excerpts of various classical jurists and constitutions on a number of themes. Only a small part of the original appears to survive. The work dates to about AD 320 (Liebs 1987: 151).

The quality of legal argument (if any) in these works is not always high; and the Autun Gaius has been the object of particular derision. None the less, all of these works have particular value in that they present a rare glimpse of law which has not been filtered through the eyes of Justinian.

2. Codes

The 'Codes' gather together the constitutions promulgated by various emperors, mostly arranged chronologically under different subject headings. Justinian's Code of AD 534 is discussed in section II. The other surviving Code is that of the emperor Theodosius II, published in AD 438. It was preceded by two compilations of the Diocletianic period (AD 284–305), the *Codex Gregorianus* and *Codex Hermogenianus*, neither of which survives.

The Theodosian Code contains relatively little on private law, being much more concerned with public and municipal law, administration and religion. It begins with constitutions of the emperor Constantine, well beyond the end of the period with which this book deals. For both of these reasons the following chapters make little or no use of it.

3. Epigraphic and other sources

There is a large number of inscriptions, papyri and other documentary evidence about Roman law, although much of it is fragmentary. This is invaluable for the task of understanding how Roman law worked in practice. Particularly notable are the collections of tablets from Pompeii and Herculaneum, which preserve records of business and of litigation (Wolf 1985; Wolf and Crook 1989: Gröschler 1997). They are referred to especially in chapter 5. Notable too is the archive of Babatha, which serves a similar role for the near East in the first to second centuries AD (Wolff 1980). Large numbers of papyri provide records of actual cases (see for example those on advocacy collected in Crook 1995). Finally, reference should be made to the *lex Irnitana*, the latest in a series of bronze tablets found in Spain. Discovered in 1981, it is the most complete of the various surviving municipal law codes. It is discussed in more detail in chapters 1 and 6.

These documentary sources call for the usual apparatus of epigraphical, papyrological or palaeographical skills; but on the whole the fact that they are about law does not make very much difference to the approach it is necessary to adopt to them.

II THE JUSTINIANIC SOURCES

Together the legal compilations promulgated by Justinian are known as the *Corpus iuris civilis*. There are four parts to it. Most attention is paid in this section to the Digest, which is the principal source for attempts to reconstruct the law of classical Rome.

1. The Institutes

This is an elementary work on the model of Gaius's Institutes, on which it depends heavily. It dates from AD 533.

2. The Digest

The Digest was compiled in the short period of three years between AD 530 and AD 533 on the orders of the emperor Justinian. It is a compilation made from the works of the classical Roman jurists. What the Digest compilers did was make excerpts from the classical works and digest them under a series of chapters or 'titles' in fifty books. So, for example, the first title, Digest book 1 title 1 (or *D.* 1.1), is entitled 'On justice and law' (*de iustitia et iure*) and the last, *D.* 50.17, is 'On various rules of ancient law' (*de diversis regulis iuris antiqui*). More typical titles concern such things as 'On the action for recovery of property' (*D.* 6.1 *de rei vindicatione*) and 'Hire' (*D.* 19.2, *locati conducti*).

The Digest was officially promulgated by Justinian with a constitution, *C. Tanta*, setting out some of the detail of the massive work of compilation. This excerpt from that constitution gives some sense of what was involved:

... nearly two thousand books and more than three million lines had been produced by the ancient authors, all of which it was necessary to read and scrutinize in order to select whatever might be best. . . . This was accomplished; . . . we have given these books the name Digest . . . and taking together everything which was brought from all sources, they complete their task in about one hundred and fifty thousand lines. (*C. Tanta* 1)

The compilers of the Digest preserve a reference to the source from which they took each fragment. This so-called inscription is given at the beginning of the fragment; for example, *D.* 1.1.1. pr. begins '*Ulpianus libro primo institutionum*' indicating that the fragment was taken from book 1 of Ulpian's *institutiones*. Since these references to the sources are preserved, we are able to say that the Digest contains excerpts from thirty-nine different classical jurists ranging in date from Q. Mucius Scaevola in the first century BC to the jurists Hermogenian and Arcadius Charisius of the fourth century AD. Most excerpts or 'fragments' come from a core period of the mid-first to early third centuries AD, but the distribution between authors is extremely uneven. The work of the jurist Ulpian predominates, occupying just over 40 per cent of the whole; next comes Paul; at the other extreme are jurists represented by a single fragment, Aelius Gallus, Claudius Saturninus, and Rutilius Maximus.

The precise details of how the Digest compilers worked remain uncertain and controversial. What can, however, be said with confidence was said by Friedrich Bluhme in 1820: this is the so-called 'Massentheorie'. According to this theory, the compilers divided themselves into three groups in order to read and excerpt the works of the classical jurists, which would ultimately appear under the rubric of the various Digest titles. Within each group the compilers read and excerpted the works in a fixed order. When the Digest itself was compiled, the order in which the compilers had read and excerpted the classical works was to a large extent preserved, because each group's fragments for the most part appear in a single block or 'mass'. From time to time fragments are displaced from their mass for editorial reasons, for example to place them next to fragments from another mass dealing with the same subject. Most titles within the Digest contain fragments from each of these three masses, which are generally known as Edictal, Sabinian, and Papinian, according to the type of classical work which predominates

within them. There is a fourth, much smaller mass known as the
Appendix. Modern editions of the Digest indicate which mass each fragment comes from; and the standard stereotype edition also includes a
table at the end setting out Bluhme's order (Bluhme 1820; cf. Mantovani
1987). Although this may seem to – and often does – have little relevance
to the historian, none the less attention to Bluhme's order may make it
possible to identify the original context of a fragment in the Digest
(Johnston 1997a). There is more to say about this under the next heading.

Loss of context and palingenesia

A major difficulty in using the Digest is that it consists entirely of
excerpts from jurists' works. The excerpts are arranged in books and
titles. But the context from which they were excerpted is necessarily
uncertain. This means that some caution is needed in the use of evidence, since what appears now under one heading in the Digest may
originally have been said by a jurist in connexion with something quite
different.

Here some help is at hand. Because the compilers of the Digest give
the source of each fragment, it is sometimes possible to be fairly sure
what the original context of the excerpt was. That is true in particular
of the main commentaries, those on the edict or on the civil law. There
were many such commentaries, and a comparison of their surviving
fragments indicates that they were typically lemmatic in form: that is,
they followed the order of the work on which they were commenting and
dealt with each word or topic in turn. If a fragment from the Digest can
be located in a particular book of such a commentary, it follows at least
that it is possible to limit the range of possible words or topics with which
it may have been concerned; and sometimes the actual word or topic
may be identifiable with reasonable certainty.

The fundamental work of retrieving the original context of fragments, usually known as 'palingenesia', was carried out late last century
by Otto Lenel and published in his great *Palingenesia iuris civilis* in 1889.
Lenel's work is not without flaws but, although corrections have been
suggested, it remains an extraordinary achievement and has never been
superseded. It is therefore the starting point for trying to identify what
the true subject of the excerpts in the Digest actually is.

Here is an example. In the penultimate title of the Digest, 'On the
meaning of words' (*de verborum significatione*) the jurist Paul gives a
definition of 'crops' (*fruges*) (*D.* 50.16.77). It is removed from its original
context. It might be useful to know what that was. That can be done,

since the inscription shows that the text comes from book 49 of Paul's commentary on the edict. The first step is therefore to see what Paul discussed in book 49. From the *Palingenesia* it can be seen that he was talking about water; more specifically, the interdict on water and the action for warding off rainwater (*actio aquae pluviae arcendae*), which was an action brought where the defendant had constructed something on his land which caused rainwater to damage the plaintiff's land. (This action is discussed further in chapter 4 section III.) This is not at all the obvious context for a discussion of the meaning of 'crops'. But there is a reason for it to be discussed: there was no liability under this action if the thing which the defendant had constructed had been constructed for a legitimate agricultural purpose, such as the gathering of crops (Ulpian, *D.* 39.3.1.7). In this context, it was necessary to determine precisely what 'crops' were. Paul's fragment indicates that there was quite detailed juristic discussion about the definition of this term.

Such questions may typically be of more interest to lawyers than to historians. None the less, to identify the original context in which a definition was put forward or an argument advanced may clearly be of importance in historical argument too.

Interpolations

The most notorious difficulty which faces readers of the Digest, and doubtless the one which has been the greatest deterrent to its use by historians, is the question of interpolations in the Digest (Wieacker 1988: 154–73). The problem itself is easily stated: the Digest is a compilation of excerpts made several hundred years after the works from which it was compiled were written. Just as legal texts nowadays are updated and appear in new editions, so the material published in the Digest was updated to take account of changes in the law. The problem is that for the most part we know nothing at all about the original sources, so distinguishing the old from the new is not straightforward. The problem of interpolation is therefore the question of separating out which strands in a text relate to the law of Justinian's time (the sixth century), which to the law (for example) of Ulpian's day (the early third century), and which may be attributable to any intervening period.

This is not an exact science, and it is one which was practised with such fervour and lack of self-restraint in the early decades of this century that the word 'interpolation' itself remains tarnished. Views still differ (Kaser 1972; Wieacker 1988: 154–73; Honoré 1981; Johnston 1989; Watson 1994). But the fact that there are interpolations is

incontrovertible: not only does the Digest represent a massive abbreviation of the original juristic works – as noted above, according to Justinian
it amounts to only 5 per cent of the length of the original works; but
apart from this the compilers were expressly authorized in AD 530 to
make alterations:

> . . . there is something else of which we wish you to take special account: that,
> if you find anything in the ancient books which is not well expressed or which
> is superfluous or incomplete, you should cut down excessive length, make up
> what is incomplete, and present the whole in proportion and in the most elegant
> form possible. (*C. Deo auctore* 7)

With this on the historical record, the supine approach to questions
about interpolation now in vogue is historically impossible to justify.

The sort of changes the compilers actually did make are many and
various. But some general considerations can be set out:

(1) There is evidence that the compilers approached the texts with
respect (*C. Tanta* 10), so it is not plausible to imagine that they engaged
in wholesale rewriting. Not only do the compilers religiously preserve the
inscriptions, the references to the sources from which they took fragments, but they do so even where the fragment consists of only a word
or two inserted into a continuing passage taken from another author.
Had they not been concerned about accurate attribution, the compilers
would surely just have inserted a few words without comment. (See for
example *D.* 18.1.48, four words from Paul in the middle of a passage of
Ulpian.)

(2) The likelihood in any case is that the major change has been abbreviation, so nuances and details may have been lost. Since the general aim
was to make the (surviving) texts more manageable and accessible, it is
not very likely that the compilers spent much time writing new material
to insert into the classical texts.

(3) It is in general unlikely that substantive alterations will have been
made to the texts unless there is a good reason, such as the fact that
change in the law made the doctrine of a text incorrect or the institution
with which it was concerned obsolete. Where such changes were made
by Justinian, we often have independent evidence of them.

(4) The classical jurists spent much time disagreeing with one another;
many of those disputes have been suppressed. We know this partly from
parallel texts (see below) and partly because Justinian famously
embarked on a project of resolving classical controversies, and promulgated a series of laws known as the 'fifty decisions', in which the classi-

cal dispute was laid to rest and a single pragmatic solution introduced. It is unfortunate that, owing to Justinian's insistence on establishing clear rules, we are deprived of much of the richness of classical jurisprudence.

(5) The procedural system in Justinian's day was different from that of classical times; although the Digest routinely refers to the classical formulary system, the desirability of making reference to the *cognitio* system in use in Justinian's day will have led to significant changes.

The detection of interpolations

As lawyers say, each case turns on its own facts, so there is no guaranteed method for detecting an interpolation. But a few examples of different approaches may help to give a sense of what is involved.

(1) *Parallel texts.* The Digest was intended to supersede the works from which it was compiled, which were to be destroyed. That result appears to have been successfully achieved, and so it is only in the rarest cases that we find a text parallel to the Digest fragment. Such cases are as valuable as they are rare, since they provide crucial information about the sort of changes the Digest compilers did make.

Here is an example from book 17 of Ulpian's commentary *On Sabinus*, which is preserved both in the Digest and in the *Fragmenta Vaticana*. The words which appear only in the Vatican manuscript and not in the Digest are italicized.

[Julian] says that if a usufruct has been left by legacy to a slave who is owned in common and separately left to Titius, if the usufruct is lost by one of the common owners it does not go to Titius but ought to go to the other common owner, as he alone was conjoined in the grant: *Neither Marcellus nor Mauricianus approves this opinion; Papinian in book 17 of his 'Problems' also departs from it. Neratius's view is given in book 1 of his 'Opinions'. But I think* [Julian's] opinion is correct, for as long as one of the common owners uses it, it can be said that the usufruct subsists. (Ulpian, *D.* 7.2.1.2 and *FV* 75.3)

What is striking is that all reference to an apparently lively classical controversy has been struck out and a single clear view preferred.

(2) *Inconsistency.* Sometimes texts are self-contradictory, indicating that they have been altered, but inaccurately. This is one of the convenient consequences of the fact that the Digest was compiled at great speed: there are occasional loose ends which make compilatorial intervention possible to detect. A straightforward illustration is this:

If a procurator has been appointed to defend an action, he is ordered to give security with a promise that the judgment will be satisfied. The promise is given not by the procurator but by his principal. But if a procurator defends someone, he is personally compelled to give the promise. (Modestinus, *D.* 46.7.10)

Here we are told two conflicting things about procurators. The first is an interpolation; fortunately, we know from Gaius's Institutes (*Inst.* 4.101) that it was a different kind of legal representative, the *cognitor*, who did not give the promise personally. *Cognitores* were abolished by Justinian but this trace of their existence lingers on.

(3) *Known innovation.* Sometimes we know that Justinian changed the law, because the constitution by which he did so is preserved. Clear examples are the abolition of the formal conveyance *mancipatio*, with the result that the informal method of *traditio* could be used for all property; alteration of the period of time in which ownership of property could be acquired by possession (*usucapio*); abolition of one form of real security, *fiducia*, and its supersession by another, *pignus*. (The law on these topics is discussed later, in chapters 4 and 5.) These and similar changes lead to absolutely routine interpolation: where the term *mancipatio* appears, it is replaced by *traditio*; where the reference to the period for *usucapio* appears (either one or two years in classical law), it is replaced by a general expression such as 'for the statutory period'; and where *fiducia* appears it is replaced by *pignus* (e.g. *D.* 17.1.22.9; *D.* 41.10.4 pr.; *D.* 13.7.8.3).

(4) *Language.* This is the most notoriously subjective of the possible criteria for detecting interpolation, and one that ultimately led to the downfall of the interpolationist school earlier this century. The unsoundness of the method lay principally in the fact that its practitioners believed they could identify a style and in particular a vocabulary characteristic of the classical jurists. Having identified an 'unclassical word' in one text, the practitioners of this method condemned the other texts in which the word appeared; those texts contained new words which were now regarded as suspect, and led to the condemnation of yet further texts. As Otto Lenel remarked, 'the interpolation bacillus is infectious'.

In itself, however, it seems to make sense to pay close attention to the language, style and grammar of the texts, and provided this is done by taking each case on its own merits, it seems to be a valuable weapon in the search for interpolations. Over the last few decades awareness has grown that the classical jurists have individual stylistic features; if regard is paid to these, then there is a firmer basis for assessing the likelihood of interpolation (Honoré 1981; also the much earlier work of Kalb 1890). It is true – and vital to remember – that oddities in grammar or style may reflect no more than abbreviation; it is not necessary to assume that the legal substance of the text has been affected.

In short, there is no cause to abandon hope: there are reasonably solid principles which can give some guidance in questions of interpolation.

Post-classical changes

Unfortunately, however, this is not quite an end of the matter. There remains the fact that between the writing of the classical works, mostly before about AD 230, and the compilation of the Digest in the AD 530s three centuries intervened. Did the classical works pass through that substantial period unscathed?

The answer to this question must be 'no', but the degree of alteration will be very variable. All (or nearly all) classical works will at some point have been copied from the roll form in which they first appeared into book or '*codex*' form, a process that began around the middle of the third century AD; here then is one opportunity for copying errors to be made, for the text to become corrupted, and for marginal glosses to become absorbed into it. In reality, the most popular works will have been copied much more frequently, so potentially increasing the distance between them and the original. On the other hand, some works will not have been much used, and they may well have been transmitted without significant alteration (Wieacker 1988: 165–73).

Nor can we forget about the possibility of forgery, trading off a famous name in order to maximize sales; and perhaps particularly tempting in law in order to obtain the authority accorded to the great names among the jurists. We know that such forgery happened in other areas such as rhetoric and medicine, even when the author was still alive (Quintilian, *institutio oratoria*, pr. 7). And there also survive independently of the Digest some works which can scarcely have been written by the authors to whom they are attributed, such as Paul's *sententiae*.

For these reasons, what is most important is to be able to trace the history of each work, and attempt to see whether it does appear to be genuine and whether it has been subject to annotation or reworking. This can be done only by close study of its surviving fragments. Studies of this sort attempt to identify different layers in the texts ('Textstufen'), of which in a difficult case there may be many, ranging from glosses at one date, to substantial additions at another, and ultimately Justinianic interpolation. Isolation of these elements is of course not a scientific process, but depends on arguments drawn from the language, style and structure of the work, the substantive law and level of argument contained in it, and comparison with other surviving material which can be dated. This may sound daunting, and it is. But a good start has been made in a series of studies originating in Freiburg. Here there is space only to summarize the main general points which have so far emerged from such studies.

(1) Most reworking of texts is likely to have occurred immediately after the end of the classical period, in roughly AD 250–310.

(2) It seems that the post-classical law schools of the fourth and fifth centuries AD, once blamed for wholesale onslaughts on the texts, actually approached them with restraint; their intervention is likely to have been confined to writing glosses on the texts, some of which, it is true, may have been absorbed into them. There is, however, some evidence of substantial additions to works which were used for teaching in the law schools: this applies, for example, to the 'Problems' (*quaestiones*) of Paul (Schmidt-Ott 1993).

(3) Early classical works are relatively free of post-classical reworking; they probably went through relatively few editions. This is true, for instance, of the 'Letters' (*epistulae*) and 'Books on Cassius' (*libri ex Cassio*) of Iavolenus Priscus (Eckardt 1978; Manthe 1982). On the other hand, the works of the great Severan jurists, Ulpian, Paul and Papinian, are more likely to have been subject to much reworking, in the course of regular new editions.

3. Justinian's Code

Justinian's Code was promulgated in AD 534. The Code which survives is the second edition. A first edition had apparently confined itself to excerpting the constitutions of earlier emperors. In the meantime, however, Justinian issued his 50 decisions (see above, pp. 18–19); this led to the preparation of a new edition of the Code incorporating those decisions and consequential amendments to other constitutions in the first edition.

In the Code the references to the consular dates of each constitution are mostly preserved and so are the names of the addressees. This makes it relatively straightforward to know, for example, whether a given constitution was issued in response to an individual inquiry, a request from a governor or other official, or was conceived as an edict addressed by the emperor to a particular person or persons. For the most part, therefore, it can be said that the constitutions represent real responses to real problems.

Questions about selection and interpolation can be dealt with more briefly here. So far as selection is concerned, the compilers of the Code were instructed as follows:

We specially permit them to cut out from the three Codes and subsequent constitutions prefaces which are superfluous, so far as the substance of the laws is concerned, as well as those which are repetitious or contradictory, unless they assist some legal distinction, and those which are obsolete; and to compose laws which are certain and written in a brief form; to bring them under fitting titles, adding and subtracting and even changing their wording when the usefulness of the matter demands it; to collect into one law matters which are dispersed between various constitutions; and to make their meaning clearer; provided, however, that the chronological order of these constitutions appears from the inclusion of dates and consuls and also by their arrangement, the first coming first, the second second, and if there are any constitutions without date and consul in the old Codes or in the collections of new constitutions, to place them in such a way that no doubt can arise as to their general binding force, just as it is plain that those which were addressed to individuals or a community but which are included in the Code because of their usefulness receive the force of a general constitution. (*C. Haec* 2)

This instruction makes it clear that basic sources for Justinian's Code for the period up to AD 438 were the three earlier Codes, the Theodosian Code, which contained general laws (*Cod. Theod.* 1.1.5), and the two Diocletianic Codes. The first of those Codes, the *Codex Gregorianus*, contained rescripts issued in response to the inquiries of individuals and went back as far as Hadrian and up to AD 291. This Code was itself probably based to some extent on earlier collections of rescripts. The second Code, the *Codex Hermogenianus*, appears to have been a sort of supplement to the first, covering the years after AD 291, and to have been published in AD 295 (Turpin 1985). As is clear from the constitution just cited, even private rescripts were, by virtue of their inclusion in Justinian's Code, to have general force.

The fact that Justinian's compilers relied to such an extent on earlier compilations means that in relation to interpolation two main issues arise. The first is the question of changes in the texts between their promulgation and their inclusion in the earlier compilations. Certainly once the texts of these laws had been collected into compilations or codes, there was no real scope for unofficial alterations to be made to them. It is not unlikely that the original constitutions were abbreviated, perhaps by the authors of the earlier codes or the collections on which they themselves relied. But in the absence of a parallel textual tradition the whole matter is extremely unclear.

The second point – changes made by Justinian's own compilers – is much clearer: the fact that there are often parallel texts in the Codes of Justinian and Theodosius means that the activities of Justinian's compilers can sometimes be observed. Where there is no parallel text, much the same approach has to be followed as for interpolations in the Digest (Wieacker 1988: 173–8).

4. The Novels

These are constitutions of Justinian which post-date the promulgation of the Code, the first of them dating from AD 535. Most are in Greek. They are not discussed further in this book.

III PROBLEMS IN USING LEGAL SOURCES

It would be wrong to suggest that we can tell nothing about actual practice from the writings of the Roman jurists. But the limits of such evidence do need to be clearly appreciated. What we can attempt to draw from the legal material is a picture of how or how well the law facilitated a particular activity, and how it may have influenced choices made by those involved in such activity, by favouring one approach or structure over another. But the results of that sort of investigation do not go much beyond hypotheses, which require to be verified or falsified by looking at the evidence of actual practice, so far as there is any.

A few obstacles in the way of historical investigation require specific mention.

1. Are the legal cases reported in the Digest real or imaginary?

A common concern about the evidence preserved in the Digest is that it is not historical but instead a collection of carefully crafted hypothetical cases designed by the jurists to illustrate legal doctrines. There is some truth in this, but it is certainly not the whole truth. It would in any case be surprising if the jurists designed hypothetical cases which were entirely remote from the realities of life in Rome.

Our difficulty arises partly from the fact that the jurists do not concern themselves with whether or how the facts in a case can be proved. They simply discuss the law on the assumption that the necessary facts can be established. Many of the opinions of the jurist Q. Cervidius Scaevola include the phrase 'on the facts as stated' (*secundum ea quae proponerentur*). But that limitation, although not express, must apply to the opinions of others too. This reluctance to engage with the facts does tend to distance the jurists' discussions from untidy reality. But it does not mean that they were not advising in real cases.

How are the real cases to be distinguished from the imaginary? Some guidelines are possible. The most important point is to be aware of the nature of the juristic work from which the case is taken. Some works are self-consciously devised as books of problems (*quaestiones*) and, while their underlying assumptions may (or, less likely, may not) be realistic, they need not arise from a real inquiry or reflect a real practical concern. Other works are designed for instructing students (*institutiones*); here too the emphasis may not be on real cases but on communicating elementary points, which may involve striking examples (Gaius, *Inst.* 3.97a–98).

On the other hand, there are many works which do no more than collect the legal opinions – *responsa* – given by the jurists in actual cases. These tend to appear under the title *responsa* or *digesta*. Here it is usually reasonable to presume that what we are faced with is a real opinion on real facts, delivered to real people. That impression is supported by the jurists' tendency (referred to in chapter 1) to give a bare recital of the facts, based on which they then briefly express an opinion about the law. It certainly seems doubtful that some of their more unhelpful opinions would have been invented; and much more likely that they are real cases (Scaevola, *D.* 34.1.19 and *D.* 33.7.20.9).

In some cases the impression that these are real cases is confirmed by the fact that the parties' names are preserved; in a few cases, where the same case is reported in the Digest more than once, we can see that the real names have been preserved in one report but replaced by typical stock names such as Lucius Titius and Gaius Seius in the other (Scaevola, *D.* 32.38.4 and *D.* 32.93 pr.; *D.* 34.3.28.4 and *D.* 34.3.31.2; *D.* 35.2.25.1 and *D.* 33.1.21.1; also *D.* 14.3.20, where the real names are preserved in the document quoted but replaced in the narrative, and *D.* 45.1.122.1, where the slave of Seius is transformed into the slave of Lucius Titius). This means of course that it is wrong to conclude from the use of stock names that a case in which they appear is a hypothetical one.

There are rather few works which purport to record actual legal proceedings and their outcomes; one of the few is Paul's *decreta*, which records decisions pronounced by the emperor (see, for example, *D.* 29.2.97, cited in chapter 1; *D.* 36.1.76.1; *D.* 49.14.50).

Sometimes too, though rarely, a case is expressly said to have arisen in practice (*ex facto*: Paul, *D.* 2.14.4.3). A particularly interesting example is given by Ulpian, because it indicates not merely the involvement of the emperor, and of the praetor, but also that of the jurist himself in giving advice to the praetor:

... I know from an actual case (*ex facto*) that when the Campanians had extracted a promise from someone by duress, a rescript was issued by our emperor that that person could ask the praetor for the promise to be set aside, and in my presence as assessor the praetor decreed that he could either have an action against the Campanians or else a defence against their action. (*D.* 4.2.9.3)

There will continue to be difficulty in weighing up cases which neither state that they are real cases nor come from any of the genres of Roman juristic writing discussed above. Unfortunately this applies to a significant proportion of the Digest.

The question whether the cases in the Digest are 'real' is part of a larger question. Books about law do not necessarily give a clear picture of law on the ground. A sense of tradition and a respect for authority mean that lawyers fondly continue to use old categories or institutions; for the historian, there can be difficulties in drawing conclusions about the state of society at a particular time from the existence of a particular legal rule. For example, the classical jurists rigorously adhered to a distinction between two types of property, *res mancipi* and *res nec mancipi*, which had to be conveyed by different methods; but at the same time they devised new remedies which meant that if you used the wrong method it did not matter very much (see chapter 4). It is true that in this instance the lawyers were luxuriating in traditions and distinctions for their own sake. But they did not allow that to impede the practical working of the law.

In practice, too, lawyers with experience in court know that there are legal arguments which seem perfectly all right on paper but which no court is ever going to apply. There are laws about offences which no prosecutor is ever going to try to enforce. Can we suppose that there is a good fit between what we read in the books and what really happened?

The answer to this has to be that we cannot. The lively and continuing debate about whether most Romans made wills or died intestate is itself evidence of how little the many books of the Digest devoted to the law of succession can actually tell us about what was happening in real life (Daube 1965; Crook 1973; Cherry 1996). Sometimes we can rely on records of actual cases, and on rescripts answering real inquiries; and we can make as much use as possible of such other evidence as there is. But the link between theory and practice can be forged only by records of actual events; and much of the Digest is material of quite a different sort.

2. *Bias towards legal problems*

It is impossible to use the legal sources to gauge the frequency of a problem. To take an obvious example, there is a lot of law in the Digest about divorce and very little about happy marriages. But this indicates nothing about divorce rates, and reflects simply the fact that in this context most legal problems arise on the point of divorce. This is a crass illustration. But historians often fail to observe the rule to which it points: that the legal sources can indicate which problems arose, but not how often or how pressing they were.

Not only is there a bias in the sources towards issues which cause legal questions to arise, but there is also a bias towards questions which are legally difficult or interesting. Take the peculiarities of a particular type of legacy, which could be left to the testator's heir (legacy *per praeceptionem*; Gaius, *Inst.* 2.216–23). The fact that this legal institution is discussed at great length and in minute detail tells us more about what interested the jurists than what the Roman public chose to write in their wills.

It follows that in order to obtain a reliable historical picture it is particularly important to supplement the evidence of the legal sources with such things as literary, archaeological, epigraphic or other documentary evidence. Familiarity with a wide range of sources is therefore necessary. In the following chapters some attempt is made to use evidence other than the purely legal.

3. *Cause or effect?*

In legal history, a general methodological problem has to be confronted: whether it is the law which influences patterns of social or economic behaviour or it that is shaped by them. Take a simple example: suppose that Roman law has a particularly clear and coherent law of sale. Does the quality of the law bring about flourishing commercial activity? Or is it an active commercial sector which creates the demand for the law to develop such a law of contract? There is no reason why there should not be an element of truth in both of these possibilities. It seems likely that the law would not develop much sophistication unless there were a demand for it; but, as the law becomes more attuned to the needs of commerce, it can itself further the extent of commercial activity.

Here is another example. It is not surprising that actions such as that for warding off rainwater from land (*actio aquae pluviae arcendae*) developed early in Roman law (see p. 17 above, and pp. 72–3): its concern was to protect agricultural interests (there was not very much else to protect in the fifth century BC). In this case it is certainly more plausible to say that society demanded that the law should protect certain interests, rather than that the law encouraged agricultural activity. We can conclude from this example too that in some cases it may be possible to detect some broad social or economic significance in the order in which different legal remedies are created.

Further instances of these issues crop up in the following chapters; some point one way, some the other. Rather than postulate a dichotomy between the two approaches outlined initially, it seems more accurate to recognize that in law there is a complex relationship between supply and demand.

4. Legal evolution

There are similar difficulties in accounting for legal change. Developed legal systems tend to take on a momentum of their own, so that changes in the law may be brought about purely by intellectual creativity on the part of the Roman jurists, with the aim of improving or rationalizing the legal system. On the other hand, changes and developments might equally be the result of social pressure or demands to be able to do certain things within the framework of the law. Here too it cannot be said that one view is right and the other wrong; it is likely that in one case the social element will be predominant and in another the technical.

Interestingly enough, the Roman jurists exhibit an awareness of these two aspects. Sometimes they refer to the *elegantia* of a legal rule or interpretation; here they are plainly speaking with admiration of the legal craftsmanship of the institution or rule in question. At other times they speak of *utilitas*, which appears to mean the social utility of a rule, its tendency to promote a desirable policy rather than its logical or technical merit.

5. Conclusions

This seems a formidable catalogue of methodological problems; so formidable that one might expect this book to end right here. The aim of this chapter, however, has not been to deter. Instead it has been to give a broad outline of some of the difficulties peculiar to legal sources and some of the methods developed over the years for trying to minimize them. Taking due account of these should make it possible to construct valid arguments from the legal sources, and to see the flaws in those advanced by others (for example in the following chapters). Perhaps, in a single sentence, what it all amounts to is this. To write history using the legal sources alone is inadvisable; whenever possible other evidence should be employed too.

CHAPTER 3

Family and inheritance

This chapter gives a sketch of the Roman family, slaves, and succession.

I THE FAMILY

1. Paternal power

Roman law divided free citizens into two classes: those who were independent (*sui iuris*) and those who were dependent on another (*alieni iuris*). The Roman family was patriarchal: all power was vested in the paterfamilias, who was the senior male ascendant. So a child (at least as long as he or she was legitimate) was subject to the power of his or her paterfamilias, whether father, grandfather or great-grandfather. Paternal power (*patria potestas*) was in principle lifelong, so that in principle a man who had already become a grandfather might still be subject to his father's power, and become independent only late in life.

It is true (as we shall see below) that there were ways of mitigating the consequences of the fact that all power was vested in a (possibly) elderly male. None the less, this was power of an extraordinary degree, and for those subject to it represented impotence of an extraordinary degree. *Patria potestas* goes back at least to the Twelve Tables (*c.* 450 BC), and it is clear that in the early republic the powers of the paterfamilias were extreme: a power of life and death over those in the family; power to decide whether newborn babies should be accepted into the family or exposed; power to sell surplus children. Even by the later republic such primitive barbarisms no longer survived. But paternal power remained significant because of two much more practical considerations: the paterfamilias owned all the family property, and none of his dependants could own anything; everything acquired by them automatically vested in the paterfamilias.

This is very remarkable. As has been pointed out, if you had a long-lived paterfamilias, you might still be in his power when sixty-five and he was eighty-five (Daube 1969: 75–91). Still you would be able to own nothing. This seems surprising by comparison with the ages laid down for the holding of public office: in the later republic the minimum age for election to the praetorship was thirty-nine and to the consulship forty-two (both ages were later reduced). Leading public figures might therefore still have been in paternal power and unable to own anything (Paul, *D.* 1.7.3). The question arises how the Romans coped with this apparently inconvenient legal rule.

In general – to recall chapter 2 – it seems highly unlikely that the Romans would have retained this system unaltered if it really caused extraordinary inconvenience; let alone that they would have boasted of it, as Gaius does (*Inst.*, 1.55), as an institution peculiar to Roman society.

The problem will have been less universal than the picture presented so far may suggest. Recently historians have made use of funerary inscriptions recording ages at death as well as demographic tables to work out questions of life expectancy and mortality in Roman society. These investigations suggest that life expectancy was low, as is generally the case in pre-industrial societies. Estimates are that probably only a quarter of men in their early thirties were still in power; and only one in ten forty year-olds would still be in power and so unable to own any property (Saller 1994). So this is a corrective to the basic picture, and indicates that the consul who was still in power must have been the exception rather than the rule. None the less, such cases did occur. The jurists are careful to explain that paternal power applied only to matters of private law, so that a magistrate who was in his father's power had no obligation to obey him in official matters (Pomponius, *D.* 1.6.9).

Two other factors are worth mentioning. The first is the *peculium*, a fund of property made available to the dependent son or daughter (or to a slave). It is fundamental to the *peculium* that it remained the property of the paterfamilias and could be withdrawn at any time. But the person to whom it was granted had full powers of disposal over it until such time as it was withdrawn. *Peculia* could be large: they were not just pocket money or allowances. There are plenty of texts in the Digest which speak of *peculia* which contained slaves who themselves had *peculia* which contained further slaves: the highest *peculium* in this hierarchy might be of very significant value. Indeed precisely because *peculia* might be large and employed in the workings of Roman commerce, most discussion of them is left until chapter 5. It is clear that the grant of a substantial *peculium* would render more or less nugatory the fact that, strictly speaking, a person still in paternal power could own nothing.

A further significant development was the creation by the emperor Augustus of the *peculium castrense*, a fund consisting of any earnings or booty acquired by a son in the course of military service. This was a radical break with principle, since the father had no interest in this type of *peculium*, at any rate during the son's lifetime, and the son could even leave it by will. Clearly, this was a piece of social engineering rather than the coherent development of private-legal principle; and it has been suggested that the aim of this innovation was to encourage recruitment to the army. If that is right, however, it does rather suggest that the inability to own property as a dependent son was a genuine difficulty. The principle of *peculium castrense* was extended in the fourth century AD to earnings from public service (*peculium quasi castrense*) and to property inherited by a child on the maternal side (*bona materna*). The trend was therefore slowly but decisively in favour of increasing the dependent child's proprietary capacity.

A second possible corrective to our picture is emancipation, voluntary release from paternal power. The Twelve Tables contained no provision for ending paternal power voluntarily; they only provided that a son should be freed of his father's power if his father had sold him three times. (Three sales of the same son were possible because each time – until the third – he was released from the buyer's control, he would automatically fall back again into his father's power.) The Roman jurists devised a method of bringing paternal power to an end by arranging with a compliant buyer for the sale of a son three times in succession.

Accordingly, it was possible to terminate paternal power prematurely, although this would have to be with the paterfamilias's own agreement. While the juristic invention of this scheme for emancipation may suggest a social demand for it, there is not much more evidence to support that. (One might imagine that the real tyrants would neither grant a *peculium* nor agree to emancipation.) Such evidence as there is is finely balanced. Some makes it sound as if emancipation was a punishment: it broke the family tie, a fact which may have been of great consequence in a society as obsessed as Rome was with family pedigree and ancestors. It had the additional disadvantage that, if the paterfamilias died without making a will, the emancipated children had no claim on the estate (although this restriction was removed by the praetor). But there are also signs that emancipation was used as part of a strategy of planning for the future of the family as a whole, by making separate provision for, rather than punishing, emancipated family members, and this strategy was not necessarily associated with financial embarrassment (Gardner 1998: 6–113). So, although we have no way of knowing how common emancipation actually was, there is no reason to assume that it was routine. Instead, it might be called into service for any of a variety of purposes, positive or negative.

2. Adoption

It was possible to adopt people into paternal power. There were two different procedures, depending on whether the person to be adopted was at the time in power or independent. Where the adoptee was in power, it was necessary to go through emancipation proceedings in order to terminate the first power, and then for the adopter to claim the adoptee as his own. This was done in an undefended legal action, judgment in which established the new paternal power.

Where the adoptee was independent, the adoption (*adrogatio* was the technical term in this case) affected the whole property and any dependants of the adoptee; in essence it was the takeover by one family of another. This was allowed only after inquiry by the pontiffs, and only if the acquiring paterfamilias needed an heir and successor and could not provide his own (a requirement which was interpreted as meaning that he was aged sixty or over, or unable to reproduce). This background explains too why anyone would agree to such a thing: the prospect of succession was the allurement. Adoption, like emancipation, is therefore to be seen as one of the devices open to a paterfamilias to plan for the future of his family and his estate: just as emancipation could be used to reduce the number of those in paternal power, so adoption could be used to increase it (Gardner 1998: 114–208).

In each case the point of adoption was to create a new paternal power. For that reason women could not adopt.

3. Marriage

Marriage in classical Rome was more a secular than a religious matter. Its main legal effect was that children born within it were legitimate, Roman citizens and subject to the paternal power of their father; that is the context in which Gaius's Institutes discusses it (*Inst.* 1.55–6). It will be enough to summarize the requirements for valid marriage very briefly. First, there must be capacity (*conubium*), which most Roman citizens and certain others had once they were of age, twelve in the case of girls and fourteen for boys, provided the marriage did not fall within the prohibited degrees of relationship. Second, there must be consent by the parties to the marriage, and any party who was still in paternal power needed the consent of the paterfamilias. The need for his consent was gradually watered down, so that he could not obstruct the marriage, although the dates are a matter of uncertainty. In any event, demographic considerations suggest that, when they married, women would typically be in their late teens and probably half of them would by then be free of paternal power; while only a quarter of men, who typically married in their late twenties or early thirties, would when they married still be in power (Saller 1994: 25–41; Treggiari 1991: 398–403).

A striking difference between modern and Roman expectations is that in Roman law marriage had no effect on property. A strict regime of separation of the spouses' property was preserved. Just as husband and wife, if still dependent, remained in the power of their respective patresfamilias, so too, whether the spouses were dependent or independent, marriage had no effect on the ownership of property on the two sides of the family. Legislation, the *lex Cincia* of 204 BC, made gifts between spouses void. The purpose of this was clearly not to discourage birthday or anniversary presents but to prevent large capital settlements being made from one side of the family to the other. The jurists expended a good deal of effort on exploring the ramifications of this prohibition (*D.* 24.1).

The only exception to the rule that no property must pass from one side of the family to the other was the dowry (*dos*; Treggiari 1991: 323–64). This was property provided by or on behalf of the wife, for example by her paterfamilias or by relatives or friends. It appears to have been regarded as a social duty, incumbent presumably on close family, to provide a dowry (Julian, *D.* 12.6.32.2). The dowry was owned by the husband during the currency of the marriage, but a number of restrictions were placed on his free use of it. The first of these – which is also interesting as an illustration of the sort of property a dowry might contain – was a statute of Augustus, the *lex Iulia de fundo dotali*. It provided that the husband could not sell land in Italy which belonged to the dowry without his wife's consent (Gaius, *Inst.* 2.63).

The Digest gives a good deal of detail about the rules for dowries. The key point, however, is that the rules laid down by the law were only residual: they applied in the absence of contrary agreement by the parties. The size of the dowry, according to the jurists, ought to reflect the standing and wealth of the husband and wife (Celsus, *D.* 23.3.60; Papinian, *D.*

23.3.69.4). But it is clear enough that negotiation of the amount of a dowry and the terms on which it was to be returnable reflected the relative statuses, and therefore the bargaining positions, of the families which were being linked by the marriage. For example, one possibility was that the dowry would be valued at the outset of the marriage (*dos aestimata*) and the husband would be under an obligation to return that value at the end. Ulpian points out that, at least so far as items which suffered wear and tear were concerned, this was an unfavourable arrangement for the husband (*D.* 23.3.10 pr.). But he might have no choice but to agree to it. (Incidentally, it is interesting that Ulpian's view of this as an unfavourable agreement apparently assumes a low rate of inflation.)

While it is therefore not possible to generalize about the value of dowries, there is at least some reason to think that the typical dowry was a relatively small, though not negligible, contribution towards supporting the wife, her children, and her slaves in the matrimonial home (Saller 1994: 204–24). It was not, for example, as in some early modern societies, an advance to the daughter at the time of her marriage of her whole prospective share of her parents' estate. But the evidence that dowry was sometimes paid in instalments certainly makes it clear that it was a settlement of significant capital, and Cicero's difficulties in raising the necessary funds are well documented (Alfenus, *D.* 23.4.19; Cic., *Att.* 11.2.2; 11.23.3; 11.25.3). A further pointer towards the dowry's being significant but less than a daughter's full entitlement is the fact that, if she made a claim on the intestate estate of her father, the amount she had already (indirectly) received by way of the dowry was taken into account. If it is right, then, to take Roman dowries to have been relatively modest, this may have been not least because marriage was not necessarily a stable relationship, and it therefore did not make much sense to put substantial amounts of property at stake. Which brings us on to divorce.

4. Divorce

The Roman notion of marriage was that of a continuing contract entered into by consent; the corollary was that when consent came to an end, so did the marriage. Agreements to other effect were void (*C.* 8.38.2 of AD 223). Although initially the paterfamilias of the husband or the wife was able to initiate their divorce, by the second century AD his power to terminate a harmonious marriage was evidently limited (Ulpian, *D.* 43.40.1.5).

Moralists probably exaggerate how common divorce was. The facts are hard to ascertain (Treggiari 1991: 435–82). But it may well be that divorce in classical times was relatively common. No stigma apparently attached to it. Unilateral repudiation of the marriage was enough to end it; approved words for divorce were such things as 'keep your things to yourself' or 'look to your own things' (Gaius, *D.* 24.2.2.1). Under Augustus a requirement of seven witnesses to a divorce was introduced. The grounds for this seem to have been primarily so that it could be ascertained whether children were legitimate; whether the conduct of either spouse constituted adultery, as to which Augustus introduced strict penalties; and whether Augustan statutory rules penalizing the unmarried (or those who did not remarry quickly enough) were applicable. After the rigid and sometimes bizarre rules of the archaic period, classical law made no attempt to list the grounds on which divorce could be sought. In Britain and elsewhere the trend is in the same direction: the law has moved from insisting on fault as a ground for divorce to founding on the irretrievable breakdown of a marriage as grounds for terminating it. Although the Roman jurists do not spell out any rules about grounds for divorce, literary sources do suggest that a substantive reason for divorce would usually be expected (Treggiari 1991: 461–5). The effect of divorce on the dowry might anyway reduce the attraction of divorcing your spouse without any reason at all.

Major questions which arise in modern divorces did not do so in Rome. Since the husband (or his paterfamilias) had power over the children, he was in principle responsible for the custody of the child. This was reflected in the rules about return of the dowry, discussed immediately below. In practice other arrangements might no doubt be made; but the legal responsibility was clearly that of the paterfamilias.

Since marriage itself had no effect on the spouses' property, divorce had none either. There was only the case of the dowry to resolve. As already mentioned, agreements about the fate of the dowry are likely to have been common. Two types of agreement frequently mentioned are *dos recepticia*, an agreement that all the dowry was to be returned to the donor whatever the circumstances of the end of the marriage; and *dos aestimata*, already mentioned, where the husband (or his heir) was under an obligation to return property to the value of the initial dowry at the end of the marriage.

In the absence of agreement, the rules were complicated and will not be discussed here. What matters is the broad principle that, if the wife survived, the dowry should go back to her (Paul, *D.* 23.3.2). The notion lying behind this is that she should have a fund to provide a dowry for her in the event of remarriage. Since the dowry was the property of the husband, it was necessary to have an action to recover it from him when the marriage was over. This was called the *actio rei uxoriae*. In that action, account would be taken of various deductions which the law authorized the husband to make. The main ones were that the husband could retain a sixth for each child up to three, if his wife had initiated the divorce, but not if he had done so himself; he could also retain a sixth for moral reasons, notably adultery. Lesser misconduct was penalized by the retention of only an eighth.

These rules meant that even a wife who was 'penalized' to the maximum extent by having deductions made for three children and immorality would still get back a third of her dowry. She would need it: she would expect to remarry (and statute imposed penalties if she did not); and given that older women usually had to have rather more attractive dowries, it could well be necessary to top the dowry up at least to the level at which it had started. There is no doubt that this system was very much in the husband's rather than the wife's interests: it did not make it possible to penalize him effectively for immorality.

5. Tutors for those under age

A further consequence of the remarks already made about life expectancy and mortality rates is that there would be a relatively large number of children who were not yet of full age – which was the age of puberty, taken as twelve for girls and fourteen for boys – but who were already independent owing to the death of their paterfamilias (Saller 1994: 181–203). The law required them to have tutors until they came of age.

It seems that the original reason for insisting on tutors had less to do with the welfare of the children than with the welfare of their property. The law of succession is discussed later in this chapter, but it is important to note here that, until a child reached puberty and was therefore capable of producing his or her own children, his or her nearest 'agnate' (relative related through the male line) had an expectation of succeeding to the property in the event of the child's death. It was important therefore to have a tutor to ensure that the property was not squandered or dissipated because the child was cheated or defrauded. It is no accident that the person who would become tutor if nobody had been appointed by the paterfamilias in his will was the nearest agnate. In the last resort, the praetor would appoint a tutor for a child who did not have one (*lex Atilia*, before 186 BC).

The tutor was responsible for the administration of the child's property: investing property; raising or defending legal actions, and so on. This was serious business: the tutor's duties of investment alone were fairly onerous. As one would expect, the proper objects of investment had to be secure and not speculative: in short, land. It was permissible to have money on deposit, but basically only for the purpose of accumulating it to buy land; failure to take a suitable opportunity to buy land meant that the tutor was liable for interest on the sum he had not invested (Ulpian, *D*. 26.7.5 pr. and 7.3). Since the return on land was not particularly high, it is clear that the point of this liability for interest was not to maximize the child's income but to maximize the safety with which his or her assets were invested.

In addition to duties of administration, in the case of older children the tutor was responsible for authorizing certain actions. Authorization did not apply to young children, since it was possible only if the child was of sufficient age to understand what was involved. The child was able without authorization to perform acts which benefited him, but not any that harmed him, so he could acquire property or benefit under a contract; but no obligation was enforceable against him. In such circumstances, of course, nobody would willingly deal with a child. This disequilibrium was corrected in part by the praetor's preventing a child from enforcing a bilateral contract against the other party, unless he was prepared to perform his own part. For example: in the contract of sale the child could not sue for the price of goods unless he was prepared to deliver them. More generally, however, the solution to this disequilibrium was found in authorization: a transaction authorized by the tutor could be enforced against the child.

There was a gradual build up of remedies which reflect an increasing concern for preservation of the child's interests against the tutor's. Not only had every tutor (except one appointed by the paterfamilias in his will) at the outset to give security for good administration of the child's property; he had also to produce accounts of his dealings with the property, and, when the child attained full age, was exposed to the possibility of legal action. One action, the *actio de rationibus distrahendis*, applied only where there was fraud, such as embezzlement by the tutor; clearly a fraudulent tutor had only himself to blame. But a much more serious threat was the *actio tutelae*, which dates back to the late republic: here the tutor was liable for fraud but also for gross negligence; and by the late classical period the tutor might evidently be liable for any careless or negligent act in administering the child's estate (Papinian, *D.* 26.7.39.3, 7, 13–14; Kaser 1971: 365–6).

This being so, it is not altogether surprising that people began to look for excuses not to be tutors, and if at all possible not to accept appointment as tutor in the paterfamilias's will. The jurists wrote books entirely devoted to suitable excuses for not being tutors, such as holding high office, age, chronic ill health, incompetence, or having three children (those killed in battle counted towards the total). The point is that the law of excuses was worked out in detail (see *D.* 27.1). The task was clearly unattractive.

6. Tutors for women

Boys were released from having a tutor at the age of fourteen. Although girls came of age at twelve, they were not then released from having a tutor. A woman of any age had still to have a tutor. What happened at age twelve, however, is that a girl ceased to have a tutor of a serious sort and acquired one whose role was in comparison much watered down. A woman's tutor had no need to administer anything, so his functions were limited to authorization. Even that function was relatively restricted, since a woman could perform many legal acts without it: for example, convey property informally (although not by formal conveyance); give a valid receipt. But she could not make a will, free her slaves, or do any other formal acts.

Authorization in this context was more or less a formality. In almost all cases a woman could compel her tutor to give his authorization; or it was possible, if the tutor was away, for however short a period, to change tutors to somebody more compliant. This is what lies behind the remark in Gaius's Institutes that authorization in the case of women is a mere matter of form (*Inst.*, 1.190). For precisely that reason, the *actio tutelae* was not available against the tutor.

From the time of Augustus a woman could be released from having a tutor by performing her civic duty, which meant having sufficient children (three for a free woman, four for a former slave). This seems to be connected with a concern for maintaining the birth rate and so also the strength of the army. Given that having a tutor was such a modest inconvenience, it is hard to see why this incentive should have had any serious impact.

It is worth making three more points about the position of women.

(1) That women's tutorship was not very burdensome, or that women in significant numbers were now no longer subject to it, is suggested by the *senatus consultum Velleianum*, a resolution of the senate of the mid-first century AD which provided that women should not guarantee the debts of any other person (Crook 1986b). The jurist Paul says that this is because such guarantees imperil the family property (*D.* 16.1.1.1); since that is as true of guarantees undertaken by men, perhaps a better explanation is that entering into guarantees was something that it was thought, for some social or cultural reason, that women simply ought not to do. The *SC Velleianum* was interpreted fairly strictly: it applied only to obligations undertaken on behalf of someone else; and only if the creditor knew that that was the case; and it did not apply where value was given, for instance, if the woman undertook the obligation in reciprocity for an obligation she owed to the creditor (Paul, *D.* 16.1.11–12 and 24; Callistratus, *D.* 16.1.21). For these reasons, it is doubtful whether the existence of this rule prejudiced a woman's freedom to contract to any significant extent.

(2) The traditional view of Roman law was that women had tutors; they could not be tutors (Papinian, *D.* 26.2.26 pr.). But as women increasingly came to be free of their tutors, it was less obvious that they should have nothing to do with looking after the property and interests of their children. There is some evidence that – without their actually becoming tutors – this happened. Some of the evidence is provincial; but there are hints of the same thing in Rome, at least where the father of the children had authorized this (Papinian, *D.* 3.5.30.6; Ulpian, *D.* 26.7.5.8; Chiusi 1994; Cotton 1993).

(3) Many women would be free of paternal power at an early age. On the whole, they had the same rights of succession as men (Crook 1986a). It is true that a statute of 169 BC, the *lex Voconia*, imposed restrictions to the effect that a woman could not be heir to a person in the first census class; and that nobody could by gift or legacy receive more than the heir under the will. But these restrictions appear to have been evaded (Cic., *de finibus* 2.55) and certainly by Augustus' day they do not seem to have had any effect.

Once free of paternal power and in possession of her inheritance, a Roman woman was constrained only by the formality of having to have a tutor. And that was pure formality. The conclusion is surely that in Rome women were unusually financially independent.

7. Guardians

It remains to say a few words about guardianship (*cura*). Two types are attested early (in the time of the Twelve Tables) but in detail are obscure. The first is care of the insane: they were placed under the care of their nearest agnate. Later on, the praetor was responsible for appointing a *curator* if there were no agnates, or they were for some reason suspect. Once again, considerations about preserving property lay behind this institution. It is tempting to imagine that, as in Victorian novels, the power to have somebody confined as insane would have been abused. But we do not seem to have any evidence about this.

The same aura of mystery surrounds another institution open to risk of abuse: the care of spendthrifts. They too could be placed in care so as to curtail their prodigality. But here too the workings of the institution are deeply obscure.

Better attested in classical law is the *cura* of minors, those who had out-grown having a tutor but were still young. This applies essentially to males, since women were anyway subject to continuing tutorship. Fourteen was an early age to acquire full legal capacity, so something more was needed.

Here too we see a counterpoint between the introduction of rights and remedies. If the law had simply treated minors as adults, and left them to take the consequences of their ill-advised actions, there would have been no need for the *curator*. But in fact Roman law introduced pro-tection for minors under twenty-five, if advantage had been taken of them. Some of this appears to go back to an early *lex Laetoria* (around 200 BC), about which little certain is known. In any event, in his edict the praetor made available to minors, if someone had taken advantage of their inexperience, a remedy called *restitutio in integrum* ('restitution of the status quo', in other words revocation of a transaction). This was not for the case that a minor had made a bad deal, but where there was trick-ery or genuine exploitation of inexperience. The remedy was not auto-matically available but was granted by the praetor on a discretionary basis (Ulpian, *D.* 4.4.16 pr.). The problem was that the very existence of this remedy created uncertainty about whether a transaction was really valid or was liable at some future point to be challenged and revoked. While doubt persisted, the only reasonable course can have been to refuse to have any dealings with those who were or appeared to be minors.

At this point the law intervened once again, to create the device of the *curator* or guardian. Initially, a guardian was appointed *ad hoc* and only for isolated important transactions, but by the late second century AD it seems to have become common to have one for the whole period until the age of twenty-five. The point of the guardian was to protect not just the minor but the people dealing with him, since if a transaction had been entered into with his advice, it would be difficult or impossible for the minor to get it set aside.

This is an interesting example of legal evolution. The old law seems to have been content with tutorship and to have subjected males over fourteen to the same rules as any adult. This perception changed, and means of relief were introduced in certain circumstances for those over fourteen. But this shift of the law towards protection of the young had ultimately to be balanced by the creation of *cura*, to bring the law back into equilibrium. For without that equilibrium, the minor too was in effect at a disadvantage: nobody will deal with a person who deals on such unequal terms.

II SLAVERY

The modern literature on slavery is so massive that here only the briefest account will be given.

1. Slaves

Roman law enshrines a great contradiction: on the one hand slaves were property, just like a book or a dog; on the other, they were also human, and to make full use of them required that their human characteristics – their intellect and the opportunities it offered – be recognized. These two strands of thought conflict but each can be identified throughout the law.

Slaves were property. They were bought and sold like other goods. Slave dealers had a bad reputation: the seller of a slave was required to warrant that the slave was free of defects; eventually this warranty was implied in the contract of sale (more of this in chapter 5). Much the same regime applied to cattle. Nothing could make it clearer that the slave was property than the elaborate discussions of the jurists about whether an ailment, disease or impairment amounted to a defect in the goods and so a breach of contract (*D.* 21.1).

Since a slave was property, the basic notion was that the owner could do what he liked with it. Yet slaves were not purely labourers but performed much skilled work, for instance as teachers, doctors, and commercial agents. Equally, they were an extremely valuable economic resource, so that one should not get carried away with the idea that they were constantly maltreated: ill treatment of them for its own sake was self-inflicted economic harm. None the less there is every reason to think that some slaves were maltreated or inhumanely overworked.

There were, however, gradual humanitarian developments: the prohibition of excessive harshness; the requirement introduced by Hadrian that an owner should obtain the approval of a state magistrate before killing his slave who had committed crimes. Under Antoninus Pius an owner who killed his own slave was made as much amenable to justice as one who killed someone else's. On the whole, these relaxations of the original stern regime do not alter the fact that slaves are property; they are simply restrictions on the use of property, much as we find nowadays in planning legislation. A more drastic innovation, also of Antoninus Pius, was that owners whose slaves sought refuge because they were being treated excessively harshly could be forced to sell them (Ulpian, *D.* 1.6.2). This was the first time it had been possible for a slave to influence his own fate: he could bring about the expropriation of his owner, admittedly against compensation. This is indeed a recognition that the slave was a person.

There was also more direct recognition of this fact. For example, slaves were able to have quasi-marital relationships (*contubernium*). Recognition was granted to these in law; so, for example, if you bought a 'married' pair of slaves but wanted to return one as defective goods, you must return both (*D.* 21.1.35). At least this is a start. But the main catalyst for recognition of slaves as persons was provided by the self-interest of owners: to make full use of a slave involved recognizing that he or she was a person who could do things.

Here the law came up against a number of difficulties. Slaves were not people (*pro nullis habentur*) and so could neither sue nor themselves be sued. They could own nothing and anything they acquired, whether a piece of property or the benefit of an obligation, they acquired for their owners. They could not make the position of their owners worse: so they could not alienate property which belonged to their owners; nor could they bring their owners under any obligation. Accordingly, their owners could not be sued on account of their dealings either.

These difficulties are similar to those discussed earlier in this chapter in connexion with children without legal capacity and minors. So long as it was possible to sue neither the slave nor the slave-owner, nobody will willingly have done business with a slave. But that deprived slaves of a huge part of their potential utility. For that reason, the praetor intervened, to create a range of actions which could be brought against a slave-owner arising out of the dealings of his slave. These are discussed in chapter 5.

2. *Freedmen (*liberti*)*

Slaves could be freed by their owners and, if freed in due form by Roman citizens, with their freedom they also obtained Roman citizenship. After the *lex Aelia Sentia* of AD 4, however, only slaves over the age of thirty could be freed and this must be done in proper form; those 'freed' in breach of this statute became only 'Junian Latins', a lesser status which meant in particular that they had no right to dispose of their property on death. If freedmen were already second-class citizens, Junian Latins were third-class. While the size of this class is not clear, it may have been very substantial (Weaver 1997).

Freedmen were, although free, subject to a number of piecemeal and not very interesting restrictions: from the time of Augustus they could not, for example, marry members of the senatorial class. More important for present purposes is that they owed obligations to their former owners (or 'patrons'). In particular, the freedman or freedwoman was under a duty to show respect (*obsequium*) to the patron, which had some practical effects, such as the fact that he or she could summon the patron to court only with the praetor's permission; the freedman or freedwoman also had to provide services (*operae*) to the patron, the extent of which in days per year would normally be agreed at the time the slave was freed. In addition, if the freed slave died intestate the patron had certain rights of succession in his or her estate.

III SUCCESSION

1. Wills

It was open to any Roman citizen who was of age to make a will; a woman would require the authority of her tutor. The law of succession is one of the most complex areas of Roman law, and there was a large number of formal requirements which had to be met for the will to be valid. The full details need not be considered here, but included such things as formal words for the appointment of heirs and legatees; the need for the appointment of the heir to be made before any other dispositions were made; the need for children and certain others, if they were not being appointed as heirs, to be disinherited either by name or in a general clause; and attestation by a number of witnesses. What is important is that all of these requirements were requirements of form and not content. Provided the testator succeeded in complying with the form, which with legal advice need not have been difficult, the will could leave property to anyone the testator wanted.

Non-compliance with the formal requirements meant invalidity and intestacy. An interesting illustration is given by the following text:

'I, Lucius Titius, have made this will without any legal expert, observing the reason of my own mind rather than excessive and miserable pedantry; if I have done anything without due legality or skill, let the wishes of a sane man be treated as valid in law.' He then appointed his heirs. A question arose when the property was claimed on intestacy. . . (Scaevola, *D.* 31.88.17)

The jurist does not trouble to say what was wrong with the will. But the testator's plea *ad misericordiam* was evidently rejected; the will was void and therefore intestacy supervened. Given the number of pitfalls, it may be that legal help in making a will was usual.

Content of wills

Wills had to appoint an heir or heirs. The heir was responsible for continuing the deceased's family *sacra* or religious observances. The heir also succeeded not only to all the deceased's assets and rights but also to his or her obligations (so far as they were capable of surviving his or her death). This applied in particular to debts. The position of heir was therefore not merely a responsible but might also be an unprofitable one, since the debts of the inheritance might well exceed its assets and the heir would none the less remain liable to pay them in full. There is good evidence that, to spare their children these responsibilities and burdens, some testators preferred to disinherit them, and appoint someone else as heir charged with the duty of transferring property to the children, usually by way of *fideicommissum* (see below; Ulpian, *D.* 28.2.18 and *D.* 38.2.12.2). By this means the children could be spared the burdens which heirship imposed. Various technical devices were in due course devised to attempt to improve the position of the heir (Buckland 1963: 304–6, 316–19).

Apart from the appointment of an heir, the contents of a will were optional. Typically, a paterfamilias might appoint tutors for his children in minority; free some well-deserving slaves; and make legacies.

Legacies are of particular interest, because all the evidence is to the effect that these were so far from being few and modest tokens of esteem that they had actually to be curtailed by statute (Duncan-Jones 1982: 21). Much property was dispersed among many recipients; in part these, it seems, were payment for what during the testator's lifetime had been obtained through friendship and patronage. There was a series of statutes restricting the testator's power to dissipate his estate by means of legacies. Here it is enough to note the last of those statutes, the *lex Falcidia* of 40 BC, which provided that after paying legacies the heir (or heirs) must be left with a quarter of the net estate; if the total legacies exceeded that quarter, the legacies were abated in order to preserve it. This rule provided the jurists with a number of thorny technical problems, and the remnants of their discussions can be read in *D.* 35.2. What is most striking is that anybody should think of leaving more than three-quarters of his or her estate to persons other than the heirs appointed under the will.

Legacies

Several books of the Digest are entirely made up of discussion about types of legacies. They provide an invaluable picture of the sorts of property a Roman testator might have and might wish to single out and leave in a bequest. All that is possible here is to note some of the categories of legacy to which the jurists devoted particular attention: dowry; wine, corn or oil; farm equipment; *peculium*; food (*penus*); furniture; jewellery; freedom. The detailed discussions of the jurists can be found in books 33 and 34 of the Digest.

It is worth commenting in slightly more detail on four types of legacy.

(1) Usufruct is discussed in more detail in the next chapter, as an institution of the law of property. For the purposes of this chapter, what is important is that this enabled a testator to leave the ownership of his estate to one person but a legacy of the usufruct in it to another: the legatee was entitled to use the property and take its income or fruits, either for a fixed term or for life. By far the commonest arrangement was that a paterfamilias left a usufruct in his estate to his widow for her lifetime and ownership of the property to the children (*D.* 33.2).

(2) Legacies of annuities. A title of the Digest is devoted to legacies of annuities, that is payment of annual sums for the remainder of the lifetime of the payee (*D.* 33.1). The jurists construed these as a series of annual payments, of which the first was unconditional and the remainder were subject to the condition that the legatee was alive at the time

due for payment (Paul, *D.* 33.1.4). There are examples of annuities in favour of wives, children, and freedmen. It might be necessary to value the annuity in order to ensure that the *lex Falcidia* was complied with. An intriguing text of Aemilius Macer sets out how this was to be done, by making assumptions about the legatee's life expectancy at a given age: the range is from five years for those of age sixty or more to thirty years for those between birth and age twenty (*D.* 35.2.68 pr.). These assumptions, although not generous, appear not to be too unrealistic (Frier 1982; Duncan-Jones 1990: 93–104).

(3) A similar sort of arrangement was the legacy of an allowance for food or clothing (*alimenta*). The Digest suggests that this would most commonly be left to freedmen and might be for payment in monthly or annual instalments for a fixed period of years, or until the age of majority, or for life (*D.* 34.1).

(4) Legacies for purposes. Philanthropists seem to have favoured what the jurists called legacies *sub modo*, legacies for purposes to be carried out. Inscriptions as well as texts in the Digest attest a large number of these, for such things as providing games, heating public baths, paving roads, and constructing buildings, or for the commemoration of the deceased. Here is one example: 'Lucius Titius left a legacy in his will of 100 to his hometown, Sebaste, so that from the interest on it games should be celebrated in his name every other year . . .' (Scaevola, *D.* 33.1.21.3). In order to ensure the durability of such arrangements, the legatee chosen would have to be a non-natural person, such as a municipality: the legatee was then liable, so long as it existed, to perform the purpose for which the legacy had been left. In classical law, however, such arrangements suffered from the weakness that the *modus*, the purpose, could not be enforced as such: the legatee could only be forced to pay damages. (This was a general rule of the classical procedural system: see chapter 6.) There was no guarantee therefore that arrangements of this sort would be observed. In later classical law, however, it looks as if the purpose might have been enforced as such if there was a public interest.

2. Fideicommissa *or trusts*

The most versatile institution of the law of succession was the *fideicommissum* or 'trust'. This was a device which – like a legacy or succession under a will – operated only on the death of the person establishing it. But whereas appointment as heir was made directly by the testator, and a legacy was paid directly by the heir to the legatee, the trust worked indirectly, through an intermediary. The person making the *fideicommissum* would entrust (*committere*) property to the faith (*fides*) of an intermediary, for it to be conveyed ultimately to the beneficiary. The intermediary was usually, but did not have to be, the testator's heir.

Initially trusts were not recognized by the law, and the only entitlement the beneficiary had was a moral one which was not enforceable in the courts. That changed when the emperor Augustus introduced a jurisdiction charged with the enforcement of such trusts; at first the consuls were responsible for this jurisdiction. Later on, a special praetor performed the same role. An institution which had depended purely on faith and friendship now came to depend on legal obligation.

The trust was very versatile, but we can review at least its principal uses.

(1) It was used to transfer property to beneficiaries who as a matter of *ius civile* were unable to receive legacies or inheritances: for example, foreigners, proscribed criminals, those debarred under statutes such as the *lex Voconia* or the Augustan marriage legislation. There is good evidence of this in the works of Cicero (*fin.* 2.55). Although it is hard to believe that this freedom remained wholly untrammelled once trusts were actionable, there is none the less evidence of their being used for avoidance of civil-law restrictions; and a series of measures through the first and second centuries AD closing loopholes confirms the – albeit diminishing – utility of the trust for getting round inconvenient rules of civil law. There are strong parallels here not just with the development of trusts in the common law but also that of equivalent fiduciary devices such as *Treuhand* on the continent: they too were initially associated with circumvention of the strict rules of law.

(2) Under civil law the appointment of an heir was permanent. The trust, however, allowed appointment of an heir to be followed by a transfer of the whole or part of the inheritance to someone else. Gaius deals with this case 'When we have written "Let Lucius Titius be heir", we can add "I ask and request of you, Lucius Titius, that as soon as you are able to accept the inheritance you make it over to Gaius Seius." ' (*Inst.* 2.250). In this case the heir was obliged to transfer the inheritance immediately. But often the heir was asked only to transfer it after an interval; a common case was for the transfer to be made on the trustee's death (Papinian, *D.* 35.1.102; *D.* 36.1.56 and 60.8). Here the trust provided an alternative to usufruct for granting someone a life interest in property (the difference was that, whereas under usufruct the person enjoying the life interest did not own the property, under a trust he or she did, but with

the obligation to transfer it to the beneficiary of the trust). This method too seems to have been used to benefit the testator's widow during her lifetime, the property being directed ultimately to the children. There is some reason to think that this device may occasionally have been used to protect the interests of children of first marriages as against their step-mother (Humbert 1972: 207–40; but see Treggiari 1991: 392).

(3) Trusts could be imposed not only on the heir but on any person who acquired a benefit from the deceased, even if the benefit was very modest and essentially transitory, most of it being passed on to the ulti-mate beneficiary. That included heirs who succeeded on intestacy. The reasoning behind this was quite simple: 'Trusts can be charged on heirs on intestacy, since the paterfamilias is regarded as intentionally leaving them his estate on intestacy' (Paul, *D.* 29.7.8.1). Here the trust opened up a novel path: it was possible to die without making a will, yet still direct where some or all of the estate was to go.

(4) Because a trust could be charged on a person other than the heir it was able to serve purposes going beyond the generation of the deceased's immediate successors. For example, the testator might appoint someone who received land under his will as trustee under a trust in favour of a further beneficiary, whether that was a named indi-vidual or simply a member of the family. Here is one example, provided by Scaevola: 'A father prohibited his son and heir from alienating or mortgaging lands and entrusted to him that they would be preserved for his legitimate children and other relatives' (*D.* 32.38 pr.). Although in this case the son became the owner of the land, it was not his to dispose of; and its fate was already regulated by his father's will. This arrangement could extend over several generations, although classical law appears to have insisted that it was valid only so far as the beneficiaries were identifiable: the most remote beneficiaries who were still regarded as identifiable were the immediate issue of those living at the date of the settlor's death (Modestinus, *D.* 31.32.6). Those who have read a lot of English eighteenth- and nineteenth-century fiction are inclined to imagine that, as with the English entail, much of the land of Roman nobles would be tied up by this sort of device. But in fact there is little reason to believe that this was so.

3. Challenges to wills

So far the discussion has been concerned mainly with the content of wills, but the formal requirements for their validity have also been mentioned. From the late republic, however, there was also a substantive ground on which a will might fail: it might be challenged by the so-called 'complaint against an undutiful will' (*querela inofficiosi testamenti*). This was an action which could be brought by a descendant or ascendant of the testator if he or she had been left less than a quarter of what would have been his or her share, had the testator died intestate. For example, if the testator had three children, each had a prospective share of one third of the estate, and each could bring the *querela* if left less than one twelfth of it. The result of a successful claim was that the estate fell into intestacy, so the claimant received his or her full intestate share. (There might be additional complications if the claimant chose to challenge only some of the appointed heirs; in that case, the will need not be set aside in its entirety, and bequests made in the will might stand, although scaled down proportionately.)

Although it is not possible to follow through the logic of this argument (as Marcian explains in *D.* 5.2.2), the jurists appear to have taken over from rhetoric the notion that the invalidity of the will was in some sense founded on the testator's insanity at the time of making the offending dispositions. In any case, to succeed in this claim, the claimant not only had to be within the necessary degree of relationship to the testator but must also have been unduly passed over. There were perfectly good reasons for disinheriting relatives, but it is rather interesting that the jurists do not appear to discuss them. It may be that they took the high-minded view that this was a matter for the rhetoricians. Imperial constitutions, however, do go into this question: people validly excluded from benefiting include those leading immoral lives and gladiators (*C.* 3.28.19 (AD 293); *C.* 3.28.11 (AD 225)).

The *querela* is the one and only substantial restriction on freedom of testation in Roman law: a testator simply had to leave these individuals the requisite amount unless he or she had a solid reason for not doing so. But it is worth emphasizing that this tied the testator's hands only to the extent of one quarter of the estate. For the rest he or she was free. By the standards of some modern jurisdictions, the Roman regime was extremely liberal.

It is interesting that two restrictions on absolute freedom of testation – the *querela* and the *lex Falcidia* – emerged at much the same time, in the late republic. It is tempting to connect this with a breakdown of existing conventional *mores* amid the turmoil of the end of the republic. What could previously be taken for granted as social practice now had to be laid down as the law (Paulus 1994).

4. Intestate succession

Intestacy might come about either because no will was made or because the will was invalid. The second of these has already been mentioned: breach of formal requirements might render a will invalid; so might other contingencies, such as the birth of a legitimate child to the testator after the will was made.

It is a vexed question how common it was to make no will (Daube 1965 and 1969: 71–5; Crook 1973; Cherry 1996). Sir Henry Maine famously spoke of the Roman 'horror of intestacy'. There is anecdotal evidence which suggests that making a will was the norm: Cato is notoriously said to have regretted having lived a single day intestate (Plutarch, *Cato maior* 9.6). But in this respect as others he may not have been typical. Those who had nothing to leave are likely to have left no will. But the evidence seems to suggest that, motivated by horror or otherwise, the propertied classes at Rome typically did make wills. The material which survives suggests that men were significantly more likely to make wills than women (Champlin 1991: 46–9). Perhaps women were less prone to feeling horror.

It is of course a powerful incentive to make a will that, in its absence, one's property will be dispersed to people one would not wish to receive it. We must look therefore at the rules which applied for distribution of an estate on intestacy.

The rules were these. Children who became independent (that is, were released from paternal power) on the death of the deceased had the first claim to the estate, in equal shares. They were known as *sui heredes*. There might not be any (there never could be any, for example, if the deceased was a woman). In that event the next best claim was that of the nearest 'agnate' or agnates, if more than one were equally near. They were relatives who traced their relationship to the deceased through the male line only. There might also be no agnates: in the case of freedmen there never would be, and here the rule was that if the freedman left no children the patron succeeded to his estate. For ordinary free citizens, in remote pre-classical times, if there were no *sui heredes* or agnates, the property went to the *gens*. This term is sometimes translated as 'clan'. Perhaps 'extended family' is less redolent of the Scottish highlands. In the developed law the *gens* played no part, and the praetor introduced a more complicated hierarchy, in which children, including those who had been emancipated by the deceased and so were technically no longer within the family, came first; then came agnates; while cognatic relations – that is, those whose relationship with the deceased was traced either through the female or the male line – were also given a claim according to their proximity to the deceased. The appalling details of how this question was determined are contained in a text of Paul (*D*. 38.10.10). Last of all came the claim of spouses, so preserving until the bitter end the separation of their property.

What is interesting about this division is the equal treatment given to the deceased's children: no preference is given to males over females, and none to the eldest male over younger children. This system of partible inheritance must have had a strong tendency to fragment the deceased's estate, and one that may seem the more surprising in a society where possession of a particular amount of property (mostly land) was what determined an individual's membership of a given class. Various factors may have mitigated the tendency to fragmentation: for instance, making a will in which preference was shown to one or more of the children; and the likelihood that only a small number of his children would survive the deceased.

What then would be the motive for making a will? A recent study of surviving Roman wills indicates that the Roman testator was most likely to appoint his children – and particularly his sons – as heirs under his will (Champlin 1991: 107–20). But it was precisely to the children, in equal shares, that the law of intestacy directed an estate. A strong reason pointing an individual towards making a will would therefore be the desire to treat the children unequally, whether or not for the purpose of preferring the sons, and whether or not with the intention of avoiding undue fragmentation of the estate. This of course would not be the only possible reason: others would be a sort of superstition (as Maine suggested) or the desire to free slaves or pay off social obligations by leaving legacies. There does not seem to be much merit in speculating about which, if any, of these reasons would have weighed with most Roman testators most of the time.

CHAPTER 4

Property

Ownership and the means by which it is protected are the topic of the first section of this chapter. The second and third sections are devoted to land, and in particular to legal institutions providing for its exploitation and to legal remedies against the unwelcome activities of neighbours.

I OWNERSHIP

Ownership (*dominium*) in Roman law is difficult to define, and the Romans themselves did not trouble to do this. The best approach seems to be to deal with the main ingredients of ownership and from that allow the meaning of the term to emerge. The discussion in this section does need to go into some detail, in particular about the remedies available to owners to protect their property. This is not (intended to be) pure self-indulgence: it is only from the details that a reasonably accurate picture of the security of property rights and commercial transactions such as sales can be obtained.

In particular, it is important to see how Roman law dealt with the perennial problem of stolen goods: movable property gets stolen. Often it is sold to an innocent buyer. Someone has to lose. All legal systems have to decide whether the loser should be the original owner or the innocent buyer. The choice has serious implications: on the one hand, it is important to protect existing property rights; but on the other, if buyers in good faith are liable to lose their purchases, commerce may be adversely affected.

1. Acquisition of ownership

The ways in which a person became owner of a thing can be dealt with here briefly. Exotic but without great practical importance were various

ways in which ownership could be acquired *ab initio*, without a conveyance: these methods included capture of an unowned thing (such as a
wild animal or an island which had arisen in the sea); the finding of
treasure; and the creation of a new thing by the combination or trans-
formation of existing things. There is an interesting discussion of these
various possibilities in the Digest, mainly taken from Gaius (*D*. 41.1.1 to
9.2). By far the most important way of acquiring ownership other than
from the existing owner was *usucapio*, acquisition of ownership by possessing the thing for a certain period. There will be more to say about
this below.

But the usual way of acquiring ownership, then as now, was by acquisition from another person, namely the owner of the thing. A proper
conveyance of the thing would transfer it from the ownership of one
person to that of another. For certain more valuable items known as *res
mancipi* (in particular land, slaves and cattle) formal conveyance by *mancipatio* or *in iure cessio* was necessary in order to make the acquirer owner.
The details are not important here: the point was simply that greater formality and publicity were appropriate for conveyance of the most valuable items of property. Other objects were simply conveyed by delivery
(*traditio*).

It is fundamental that a person could not transfer a better title than
he had himself: somebody who was not the owner could not therefore
make a person who acquired a thing from him its owner. Money,
however, was to some extent subject to special rules, just as it is today.

Ownership in money was transferred by delivery. The normal case
would be, for example, that if the owner handed over money as a loan
(*mutuum*), ownership transferred to the borrower. (This had to be so in
the case of lending money, since the idea of the loan was not that precisely the same coins should be returned but that they should be used,
and the same value in other coins returned.)

Suppose, however, that the lender handed over somebody else's coins.
This would not transfer ownership, and the owner of the coins could
therefore claim the very same coins back (using the *vindicatio*, which is
discussed below). So far this is the ordinary rule for property. The spe-
ciality was that, if the recipient of the money spent it in good faith, the
acquirer became owner of it. Similarly, if coins belonging to different
people were mixed together, so that each could not now identify his own
and vindicate them, they became the property of the possessor (Ulpian,
D. 12.1.11.2 and 13 pr.–1; Iavolenus, *D*. 46.3.78). The consequence was
that the person who lost the ownership of the money would have to rely

on another remedy, such as a contractual action or action for theft. These rules are peculiar to money.

The critical point is that commerce demands that money should be freely transferable and that there should be no need to make inquiries into whether the person handing over the money is actually its owner. In the cases just discussed only if the precise coins are still identifiable is the owner's title unaffected; otherwise it is safe to assume that the possessor is owner.

2. Use of property

The owner in Roman law was fairly uninhibited in the use of his property, although he might be subject to statutory restrictions (such as building regulations or rules on humane treatment of slaves) as well as to restrictions imposed on the use of his land in the interests of his neighbours, whether by agreement or by the operation of law. These are discussed in sections II and III below.

3. Protection of ownership

Ownership was protected by various different remedies. Before turning to the principal remedy by which it was protected, the *vindicatio*, we should note the relevance of two other actions. The first is the action for theft, by which the owner could recover damages from a person who stole his property. The second is the action under the *lex Aquilia* (of about 286 BC), by means of which the owner could recover damages from a person who wrongfully injured or killed his property. These were important weapons in the owner's armoury.

Nevertheless, the main action with which we are now concerned is the action by which the owner could recover his property from any person who had it, the *vindicatio*. To succeed in this he required to prove that he was the owner. This sounds straightforward and might indeed be so, if he could show that he had manufactured the thing or captured it; but otherwise it would in principle require him to prove that the person from whom he had acquired the thing was then its owner. That of course would turn on whether that person had acquired from the person who was then the owner; and so on *ad infinitum*. All most inconvenient.

4. Possession and usucapio

This difficulty was avoided by relying on the concept of 'possession'. There are two important points to make about possession, both quite lengthy.

(1) Possession was different from ownership because, while ownership was based on entitlement, 'possession' was based on fact. A person who had a thing and intended to possess it was its possessor. He need not also be its owner. There is room for argument about exactly why the law chose to protect the possessor. But there is one very good reason: the best way of encouraging people to keep the peace and not to take the law into their own hands is to protect the existing possessor, whether or not he claims to be owner, until the facts have emerged properly in legal process.

The way in which possession was protected was by means of orders called possessory interdicts. This was a 'fast track' procedure under which the praetor would adjudicate on the question of possession. The rules were simple: in cases involving land, the praetor would grant possession to the person who already had it, unless he had obtained it by force or by stealth from, or with the permission of, the other party. If any of those exceptions applied, that other party would obtain possession. The rules for cases involving movable property differed in only one respect: possession was granted to the party who had had the thing for the longer period during the immediately preceding year. Again, this was subject to the exceptions of force, stealth and permission.

The procedure was simple and swift in the sense that it did not involve looking at the rights and wrongs of title and how it had been acquired. All it needed was an examination of the position between the two litigating parties: had one of them, for example, taken the thing from the other by force? If so, he must restore it to him. The result of this inquiry was correspondingly limited: the praetor could conclude only that one party had a better right than the other, but that said nothing about their absolute rights. There might be a lot of people who had even better rights than either of them. But this procedure rapidly resolved the question which of the two had a better claim to possess and so kept the peace between them.

Interdict proceedings therefore provided one way of avoiding the inconvenience of proving ownership in the *vindicatio*. If you could prove that the person who had a thing had acquired it from you, for example, only with your permission (and so had no right to set himself up as

having any right competing with yours), interdict proceedings would be
adequate to recover possession from that person. Gaius emphasizes that
it is always worth considering whether there is any interdict under which
you can recover possession: if you succeed, you transfer to the other
party the much heavier burden of bringing a *vindicatio* and the need to
prove ownership (*D.* 6.1.24).

(2) *Usucapio* was a means (as mentioned already) by which a non-owner
could become owner of a thing, by possessing it for a certain period. For
movables the period was one year, for land it was two.

To become owner by *usucapio*, a possessor had to meet certain conditions: first, he must possess; second, he must begin (though he need not
complete) his possession in good faith; third, he must have a good cause
for being in possession; and finally, he must remain in possession for the
relevant period. So a buyer who, under a contract of sale (which was a
good cause), in good faith acquired a thing from a seller who did not own
it could become its owner, by possessing it for the requisite period. This
was subject to the over-riding rule that there could be no *usucapio* of a
stolen object, a point to which we return almost at once.

The existence of *usucapio* simplified the owner's task in *vindicatio*.
Instead of needing to prove a series of owners and conveyances from
time immemorial, he could rely on proving only that he had possessed
for the necessary period under a possession which had begun in good
faith for a good cause.

Usucapio meant that the acquirer of the property was enriched at the
expense of the original owner: just as the passing of the one or two years
vested ownership in the new owner, so it divested the old one. This seems
unfair. But to this the jurists had their answers: *usucapio* was in the public
interest, so that ownership of property should not be uncertain for too
long or virtually always open to challenge, and so that there should be
some end to litigation (Gaius, *D.* 41.3.1; Neratius, *D.* 41.10.5). These seem
good points.

In fact, it is not quite clear that *usucapio*, at least of movable property,
can have had this beneficial effect of clarifying titles and rendering them
unchallengeable. The reason for this is that Roman law insisted on one
restriction: there could be no *usucapio* of a stolen object, not just by the
thief (of course) but by anyone at all. This restriction goes back to the
Twelve Tables (*c.* 450 BC). But this means that it is likely that *usucapio* of
movable property was rather uncommon: mostly when movable property ends up being sold or acquired by a non-owner it will at some point
in its history have been stolen.

In Rome, if *usucapio* was completed, the title of the possessor became unassailable. But ultimately the Roman preference was for protection of the existing title: before *usucapio* was completed, the possessor in good faith had no defence against the owner. Even after it had been thought to be completed, if the owner detected a stolen thing in the hands of a purchaser in good faith, he could still claim it back as his property. The fact that it had at some point been stolen would prevent the purchaser relying on *usucapio*. That would leave the purchaser with only a contractual claim for damages against the seller; and if the seller was himself the thief, such a claim would not be worth much in practice. Thieves are hard to find; when they are found, they find it hard to find any money.

5. Other titles to property

The topic of *usucapio* leads naturally into the question of other titles to property. The Romans were strict in saying that there was only one form of ownership, *dominium*. But in fact they created other statuses which were well protected, although they lacked the formal title of ownership.

(1) A person who acquired a thing in good faith from somebody who was not the owner was not himself the owner either, since a non-owner could not transfer ownership to him. But such a person, a bona fide possessor, was worthy of protection by the law, since he had no reason to doubt the validity of his own title to the thing. Put delphically, the good faith of the possessor in good faith consists in thinking that he is not a possessor in good faith but the owner.

By *usucapio* a bona fide possessor would become full owner in either one or two years. But, until the period for *usucapio* had run, he faced a difficulty in recovering the property if he lost possession of it. It is true that, since he was a possessor, he was protected by possessory interdicts. But he might not find any interdict of use in his case: for instance, if he had not lost possession by force, stealth or permission or (in the case of movables) if he had been out of possession for a significant period. Nor could he use the normal action for recovery of property (*vindicatio*), since this required proof of ownership, something which the bona fide possessor could not satisfy.

The solution was to provide the bona fide possessor with a modified version of the *vindicatio*, known as the *actio Publiciana*. This appears to have been introduced in the last century of the republic, possibly in 67 BC. Why precisely then is a question which cannot be answered, just as it remains uncertain whether the primary purpose of this innovation was to meet the difficulties of the bona fide possessor or the rather different ones faced by the bonitary owner (see below; Jolowicz and Nicholas 1972: 164–6). The special feature of the *actio Publiciana* consisted in asking the judge to decide not whether the plaintiff was owner now (which he was not) but whether after the period of *usucapio* he would be. That meant that the judge must hear evidence on the requirements of *usucapio* other than the period of possession: did the plaintiff acquire possession in good faith? Did he have a good cause for possession? He would also, if this issue was raised by the defendant, have to consider whether the thing had been stolen. A person who had purchased the object in good faith from a non-owner would be able to satisfy those requirements, so the judge would be entitled to conclude that he should succeed in the claim; always provided, of course, that the object had not been stolen.

It is appropriate here to point out one more concession made to the bona fide possessor: this was that, if the object he possessed bore fruit (whether literally, or in the form of the young of animals), the bona fide possessor became its owner by the very fact of its separation from the parent. Even if the bona fide possessor was successfully sued for return of the parent object, in classical law there was no obligation to hand over its fruits. The precise reason for this rule is not very clear. In some cases, such as that of crops, it is plausible to say that the rule protects the bona fide possessor's labour or investment. But in others (animals) it can only be said to be protecting his reasonable expectations. Paul puts it very broadly: the bona fide possessor is protected because he is more or less in the position of the owner (*D.* 41.1.48). In any event, this rule is a further pointer to the fact that bona fide possession was a status with significant rights and significant legal protection.

(2) For completeness, it should be noted that the *actio Publiciana* was also available to another person whose standing fell short of complete ownership or *dominium*, namely a person who acquired a thing which required formal conveyance (a *res mancipi*) from the owner but received it only by an informal conveyance: the bonitary owner. Since ownership passed in such things only by formal conveyance, the recipient was not owner. But, equally clearly, as an acquirer directly from the owner, he deserved legal protection. So much so, that if it came to *actio Publiciana* proceedings between the bonitary owner and the owner, the bonitary owner would succeed.

The *actio Publiciana* required slightly less to be proved, so it is at least conceivable that even full owners might have chosen to use it. But the main difficulty – that, owing to the exclusion of stolen goods from *usucapio*, a plaintiff may always have harboured a slight doubt about whether something was really his own – was a difficulty regardless whether proceedings were raised by *vindicatio* or by the *actio Publiciana*.

6. Some conclusions

All this may seem very technical: what does it all add up to for the purposes of the historian? There are two main points.

(1) A good deal of importance was attached to possession rather than ownership. The remedies by which any possession, and in particular that of the possessor in good faith and bonitary owner, was protected were potent. This indicates that Roman law was seriously concerned with preservation of the status quo and keeping the peace, and less so with questions of formal entitlement. It is true, of course, that the Romans insisted on formal conveyance for certain objects, and that ownership in these things could otherwise not pass. But at the same time they were prepared to innovate so as to make the difference between those types of conveyance nugatory. Gaius himself spoke of a double system of ownership at Rome (*Inst.*, 1.54); the amalgamation of the two nearly four centuries later was long overdue. The emphasis in developed Roman property law was often therefore not really on who was the owner, but on who was entitled to the protection of possessory remedies and the *actio Publiciana*.

In other respects too the position of the bonitary owner and bona fide possessor was satisfactorily protected: section III deals with remedies by which an owner could protect himself in relation to his neighbours; it is likely that all or most of these were also open to bonitary owners, although the position in relation to possessors is not always so clear (Bonfante 1926: 345–6, 380, 409, 448–9). Certainly, the actions for theft of the property and for wrongful damage to it were open to both of these people.

(2) None the less, when faced with a choice between protecting an innocent owner and an innocent possessor in good faith, Roman law opted to protect the owner. And, although *usucapio* meant that ownership of property theoretically did not remain uncertain for long, this was less than the whole truth given the exclusion from *usucapio* of stolen goods. This seems to suggest that – with the exception of money, for which special rules were necessarily developed in the interests of commerce – the Romans were relatively unconcerned about the effect of their prop-

erty rules on commercial transactions. The position is likely to have been mitigated, however, by the difficulty of proving a theft many years after it had taken place.

This section looks at the various legal devices which were used to exploit land, notably leases and usufruct. For the purposes of this section, 'land' means land together with the buildings built on it: that reflects a rule of Roman law that ownership of land carried with it whatever was built on the land (Gaius, *Inst.* 2.73). The Digest contains a good deal of incidental information about the exploitation of land. For Roman society the essential point is that land was always the primary investment (Pliny, *epistulae* 3.19.8). It is no accident that the word wealthy (*locuples*) means 'rich in land'; and it is equally clear that landed wealth might go hand in hand with low liquidity (Cic., *Att.* 16.2.2). Clearly, there are various possible ways in which land may be managed: it may be occupied by the owner, by a tenant, or in some other way, such as under a usufruct (Garnsey and Saller 1987: 71–7).

There is evidence of leasing of urban property as an investment, although probably compared with rural property this was on a small scale. The risks were evidently higher – collapse of buildings and especially fire – but the returns were commensurately greater than in letting rural property (Aulus Gellius, *Noctes atticae* 15.1.1–3). None the less, the Digest contains a good deal of evidence about urban letting (for example, see Ulpian, *D.* 5.3.27.1).

The main rental market appears, however, to have been in rural property. Although this got off to a slow start, by the time of our principal legal sources tenancy appears to have become the chief method for exploiting land throughout the Roman empire (Finley 1976; de Neeve 1984: 164–74; Kehoe 1997: 5, 156–66). For that reason, most of this section is concerned with tenancy.

1. Occupation by the owner

This does not raise any significant legal issues beyond the question of remedies, which has already been discussed. Slaves would of course be likely to bear most of the burden of work; a (free or slave) manager or *vilicus* would regularly be appointed.

2. Leases

The owner might let out his property for occupation by tenants. A lease in Roman law is a contract. It therefore generated rights *in personam*: that is, personal rights of the landlord against the tenant and vice versa. The principal obligation on the part of the landlord was to give the tenant vacant possession of the premises leased, and on the part of the tenant to pay the rent.

Until recently it was widely held that the law of lease was a paradigm of law forged in the interests of the landowning classes. One of the main reasons for this was that, to put the matter in modern terms, the tenant had no security of tenure. (There will be more to say about this later.) The truth, however, appears to be more complicated. It is too simplistic to assume that all tenants were underdogs and that the law was written in the interests of the landlords. It has recently been shown that there was a substantial urban rental sector, and that the tenants were regularly members of relatively high social classes. So much is suggested too by certain rules of the contract which do not fit at all well with the notion of the poor, exploited tenant: for example, leases were regularly for periods of several years; the rent was typically paid in lump sums at yearly or half-yearly intervals. In general, the jurists' treatment of the contract indicates that they were alive to the interests of both landlord and tenant (Frier 1980: 39–47, 174–95). And the fact that the jurists assume as a matter of course that tenants might sue their landlords does not suggest that there was a great gulf between the social or economic standing of the two parties to the contract. This is not to say that there were no poor or oppressed tenants and no slums. Of course there were: the point is rather that the jurists were mainly concerned with the workings of leases entered into by the well-to-do. The Digest therefore presents only a partial picture of Roman society.

Similarly, so far as leases of rural property are concerned, the strength of the landlord's position can be exaggerated. Columella speaks of the importance of continuity in tenancies (*de re rustica* 1.7.3), and Pliny of a shortage of tenants (*ep.* 3.19.7). Since there was certainly a lack of other possible investments, and, since there was a limit to the area the landlord could himself cultivate, the landlord had every reason to attempt to keep good tenants in place. The Digest provides instances where the question is raised of compelling a tenant to remain in occupation, and even a case where the seller deceives the buyer into thinking that the property sold is occupied by a tenant. In these cases clearly the presence of the tenant is regarded as being a good thing (Julian, *D.* 19.2.32; Hermogenian, *D.* 19.1.49 pr.; Kehoe 1997: 163–6).

The law of leases is therefore more even-handed than previously assumed. This will be confirmed by closer inspection of some of the key topics.

The landlord and the tenant

Landlords might lease premises directly to the tenants who were to occupy them. But this was not the only possibility: particularly in the case of leases of flats, we find leases of the premises as a whole to a tenant who would then enter into sub-leases of the individual flats with the actual occupiers. There are examples of this in the Digest (Alfenus, *D.* 19.2.30 pr.; Labeo, *D.* 19.2.58 pr.). The advantage from the landlord's point of view was that he had in place a manager, who had undertaken to pay a fixed rent. He therefore shielded the landlord not just from the tiresome business of dealing with individual tenants but also from fluctuations in the rent, owing, for example, to inability to let the premises fully or the insolvency of one of the occupiers. The disadvantage was of course that this security came at a price: the head landlord would receive only a proportion of the full market rent, since the sub-landlord had to have his cut. For example, in Alfenus' text, the landlord let a building for thirty, and the tenant sublet the apartments in it for a total of forty.

The same enthusiasm for making use of tenancies for management purposes is found in relation to land: there is some evidence of dividing up landholdings in order to make it easier to attract tenants to them (Paul, *D.* 31.86.1). Furthermore, rather than leave an estate to be managed by an administrator or *vilicus* who had no financial interest in it, there was much to be said for letting it to someone who did. This extended even to a landlord's letting land to his own slave (a so-called *servus quasi colonus*), who would pay the rent for it out of his *peculium* (Kehoe 1997: 156–73). The slave managed the property not under master's orders, as it were, but as his tenant, for a rent (Scaevola, *D.* 33.7.20.1).

Vacant possession

The landlord's obligation was only to provide the tenant with vacant possession of the property in a state such that he could enjoy it. Failure to do this was a breach of contract on the part of the landlord and would make him liable in damages. So, for example, the landlord was liable if the leased building had to be demolished, as well as for less drastic breaches of contract such as the blocking of daylight from a flat (Alfenus, *D.* 19.2.30 pr.; Gaius, *D.* 19.2.25.2). Similarly, if leased land was untenantable, or the farm buildings or stables in disrepair, the landlord would be liable (Ulpian, *D.* 19.2.15.1). But, provided the landlord met this obligation, the tenant was under an obligation to pay the rent.

The tenant's obligation was qualified somewhat by the development of rules for abatement of rent (*remissio mercedis*), particularly in the case of rural property in the event that the crop failed. Although the rationale underlying this doctrine is not entirely clear and controversy continues (Frier 1989–90), it seems to have become settled that where overwhelming force, *force majeure*, caused the failure of the crop, that risk lay on the landlord. The consequence was that the tenant was not obliged to pay the full rent, but the rent due by him was abated pro rata. The tenant might still be liable to make up the rent to the full amount, if future years were particularly fruitful. The sorts of events which this doctrine of abatement covered were flooding, enemy attack, and earthquake but also, much less obviously, extreme frosts and heatwaves. By contrast, where the tenant's complaint was simply that he managed to harvest only a poor crop, or that the vines leased were old and not very fruitful, he obtained no redress. He ought after all to have been aware of that when he entered the contract (Ulpian, *D.* 19.2.15.2–5, 7). The rules are summed up in a text of Gaius, which is also important for the discussion of rent in the next section:

Force majeure ought not to cause loss to the tenant, if the crops have been damaged beyond what is sustainable. But the tenant ought to bear loss which is moderate with equanimity, just as he does not have to give up profits which are immoderate. It will be obvious that we are speaking here of the tenant who pays rent in money; for a share-cropper (*partiarius colonus*) shares loss and profit with the landlord, as it were by the law of partnership. (Gaius, *D.* 19.2.25.6)

At the end of the text, Gaius refers to share-cropping, the possibility of paying rent as a proportion of crops harvested. One consequence of doing so, as he points out, is that the tenant does not carry the whole risk of the failure of the crop as he would in an ordinary lease, since what he has to pay is scaled down automatically.

Much the same approach to abatement of rent seems to have been adopted in urban leases: a difficult (because corrupt) passage of the republican jurist Alfenus Varus indicates that the tenant cannot rely on minor inconvenience (such as repair work) as a ground for withholding rent: there must be a substantial impact on his occupation of the premises to allow him to do so (*D.* 19.2.27 pr.). This text as it stands does not say how much rent could be withheld, but it is perhaps not unreasonable to assume that it would be in proportion to the part of the premises which was unusable.

To cut a long story short: freedom of contract allowed the parties to make their own bargain. They might opt to share the risk of crop failure, as in Gaius's example, or they might contract to place the whole risk on the tenant (Ulpian, *D.* 19.2.9.2). But, if they made no other agreement, the risk of *force majeure* was on the landlord. The very existence of this doctrine shows that landlords did not have the law all their own way: in certain circumstances it was appropriate for them and in practice they would probably have had little alternative but to make concessions in order to retain their tenants. That is exactly what Pliny appears to have done (*ep.* 9.37.2; 10.8).

Rent

The contract of lease of property (*locatio conductio*) involved the letting of a thing against payment in money. The text of Gaius just cited shows that at least one jurist (writing here – perhaps significantly – in his commentary on the provincial edict) was aware of a practice of paying rent in kind: the landlord took a share of the crops as the rent. The practice is also mentioned by Pliny (*ep.* 9.37.2). It seems not unlikely that this type of rental agreement was an import from the Greek East; and in Egypt it was apparently a typical form of lease. None the less, although the jurists were not wholly inflexible, on the whole they avoided discussion of the peculiarities of this type of rental agreement and confined themselves to cases of money rent (Africanus, *D.* 19.2.35.1; Gaius, *Inst.* 3.144).

There is some reason to believe that this sort of tenancy agreement was characteristic of the lower end of the spectrum: the tenants might be supplied with some of the necessary equipment, and might be supervised, sometimes by slaves, for the obvious reason that their efforts directly influenced the landlord's own income from the land (de Neeve 1984: 16–18).

Other terms

These basic contractual terms could be supplemented. Since the parties were free to fix the terms of their own contract, and clearly did so, there is little to be said for rehearsing the great variety of terms here, and much to be said for simply referring to *D.* 19.2. But a few examples may be given.

In urban leases we find such things as terms prohibiting the lighting of a fire and also (more conveniently, if less clearly) the lighting of a harmful fire (Ulpian, *D.* 19.2.11.1). In rural tenancies, the tenant would anyway be under a general duty to occupy and to keep the land in good heart, but he might also come under more specific obligations, for example to cultivate in a particular way or to build something (Iavolenus, *D.* 19.2.51 pr.; Paul, *D.* 19.2.24.2–3; Gaius, *D.* 19.2.25.3); conversely, the landlord might come under an obligation to supply certain equipment (Ulpian, *D.* 19.2.19.2).

In any kind of tenancy it was open to the parties to reinforce the contractual obligations by setting penalties for failure to comply with them (Paul, *D.* 19.2.54.1).

Termination

Since the Roman lease generated only personal rights, the tenant obtained no right to the property (right *in rem*). It follows that the tenant's position was relatively insecure. In the event of sale of the property by the landlord, the tenant had no claim on the property, and no rights against the new owner, and could therefore simply be ejected. It is true that this might involve the landlord in payment of compensation for breach of contract; but that would be little consolation to a tenant whose primary desire was to be allowed to remain in occupation. Nowadays, by contrast, under the typical lease tenants have certain statutory rights to security of tenure.

This lack of security of tenure in Roman law does appear to favour the landlord. But two qualifications should be borne in mind. First, as mentioned already, a landlord had every interest in trying to retain a satisfactory tenant. Second, the way the jurist Gaius describes sale of tenanted property does not suggest that the buyer's first act would have been to proceed with summary eviction: he says that the seller should take care that the tenant is entitled to enjoyment on the same terms under the new owner; otherwise the seller is liable to his tenant for breach of contract (*D.* 19.2.25.1). Clearly, this does not prove anything, but it counsels caution in assuming that the tenant was in practice in a fragile position.

The lease might also end by abandonment by the tenant before its full term was up. Although we do not know much about the details of this, it seems likely that the tenant would remain liable to pay damages based on the rent for the full term of the lease, unless he had a reason which justified abandonment. The only reasons the jurists discuss are related to physical deterioration of the property (Paul, *D.* 19.2.55.2; Frier 1980: 92–105).

3. Long leases

In later classical law a new form of lease is found in which the tenant does have a right to the leased property, often indefinitely, as well as to protection by interdict and a proprietary action. He therefore has security of tenure. This form of lease seems to have been developed first for leases by the Roman state or municipalities. Later law seems also to have allowed private arrangements along the same lines, normally of land on which the tenant was to build (*D.* 43.18).

4. Usufruct

Usufruct gave a person certain rights in a thing for a period, which might be either a term of years or a lifetime. The rights involved were, as the name suggests, to the use (*usus*) and enjoyment of the fruits (*fructus*) of the thing. These rights were exclusive, so the owner had no right to use or enjoyment until the usufruct came to an end. A usufruct might be over movable property or land; the present concern, however, is solely with land.

Just as leases split the exploitation of land between two people, the landlord and the tenant, each of whom enjoyed part of its fruits, so too usufruct divided it between owner and usufructuary. But the social context of usufruct was very different: the typical usufruct was left by a testator to his widow and gave her a right for life to the use of, and income from, his estate, while leaving the ownership of that property to the testator's children.

Notwithstanding this cosy family background to the institution of usufruct, the jurists developed a good deal of law regulating the respective rights of owner and usufructuary. It seems unlikely that this was simply for their own amusement, and more probable that there were disputes about precisely what the usufructuary was entitled to do. It is clear that there is a built-in conflict of interest between a person with a life interest in property and the person who will become unrestricted owner of the property when the life interest comes to an end: the person with the life interest is interested only in the short term, in maximizing income, and has no personal interest in (for example) the good heart of the land in the long term. The owner, on the other hand, will be interested in seeing that the capital value of the land is maintained and that it is not threatened by policies designed only to boost short-term income.

The usufructuary was kept in order in two ways: first, he could be held liable to the owner under the *lex Aquilia* for wrongful damage to property; second, he was required in advance to give a promise to return the property at the end of the period of the usufruct and to treat the property as a reasonable man would do. This second part of the promise enabled the jurists to enter in extraordinary detail into the question what the usufructuary was entitled to do with the property, as a glance at title *D.* 7.1 will confirm. Here it is enough to give two examples.

If trees are uprooted or blown down by the wind, Labeo says the usufructuary can use them for his own purposes and that of the villa, but he is not to use the wood as firewood if he has another source for that. I think this view is correct: otherwise if the whole estate suffered this fate the usufructuary would make off with all the trees. Labeo thinks the usufructuary can cut wood for the purpose of repairing the villa; in the same way, he says, he can burn lime or dig sand or take what is necessary for the building. (Ulpian, *D.* 7.1.12 pr.)

The usufructuary ought not to make the state of the property worse, although he may make it better. If the usufruct of a farm is left by legacy, he ought not to cut down fruit-bearing trees or demolish the villa or do anything to the detriment of the property. If it was a pleasure garden, having greenery or pleasant drives or walks shaded by ornamental trees, he must not destroy this in order, for example, to create market gardens or anything else for the purpose of profit. (Ulpian, *D.* 7.1.13.4)

From these texts it is clear that observing the standard of the reasonable man meant that the usufructuary could not go all out for profit. The cases discussed in the Digest are many and various, but in the end they come back to one point: the usufructuary must not damage the substance of the property. In a given case views might differ on whether the usufructuary's use of trees or minerals was or was not damaging the substance of the property (e.g. Ulpian, *D.* 7.1.12 pr. and *D.* 7.1.13.5). Modern views might also differ on whether the approach adopted here by Roman law demonstrated a lack of economic thinking or a welcome rejection of short-termism.

III RELATIONS WITH NEIGHBOURS

1. Boundaries

A fertile area for dispute between neighbours was the question where the boundary between their respective properties lay. The Twelve Tables had already provided an action for this, the action for regulating boundaries (*actio finium regundorum*; table 7.2; Gaius, *D.* 10.1.13). Where the boundary was simply unclear or there was a dispute about the ownership of land at the boundary, either neighbour could raise this action, and the judge would adjudicate on where the boundary lay. The consequence of his judgment might be to vest ownership in one neighbour and divest the other.

2. Servitudes

Roman law recognized a limited class of servitudes (*servitus*), rights in the property of another. The most typical example is a right of way across a neighbour's land. Of course, it was always open to the landowners to enter into an agreement that one could cross the land of the other and, if made in the proper form, it would be enforceable in contract. But such an agreement would bind only those who were party to it; and it would therefore immediately cease to be of any value if one of the landowners sold his or her land to someone else.

To overcome this insecurity it was essential that the right of way be a right not exercised against a specific person (who might change) but against a specific piece of land. This, broadly speaking, is what a servitude is: a right inseparably and permanently attached to one piece of land (the 'dominant' land) and exercisable against another (the 'servient' land). The consequence is that changes in the ownership of the land make no difference to the existence of the servitude.

The original servitudes recognized at an early stage in Roman legal development were mainly rights of way of varying extent (on foot, with cattle or a vehicle, or both of those; *iter, actus, via*) as well as the right to lead water across another's land (*aquaeductus*). It is clear that the class of recognized servitude rights gradually expanded, to include such things as the right to draw water, extract clay or lime, pasture cattle, and so forth.

The servitudes mentioned so far were known as 'rural' servitudes, probably (although this is uncertain) because as a rule they served agricultural purposes. There was another class of servitudes, 'urban' servitudes, which again were probably of use mainly in urban areas. Urban servitudes included such things as the right to light, to prevent a neighbour's building beyond a particular height, or to let water run off into the neighbour's property. Curiously enough, each of these urban servitudes appears to have had a counter-servitude: the right to obstruct light;

to build up beyond a particular height; not to have water run onto one's property. It is difficult to be sure what the right explanation for this is, but the best seems to be this. The starting point was that any neighbour was entitled to a reasonable amount of light, or to build up to a reasonable height. If a proprietor wanted to have more (more light, a higher building), or wanted his neighbour to make do with less (less light, a lower building), he would have to negotiate a servitude with him. So these servitudes and counter-servitudes represent deviations from a norm (Rodger 1972).

There is an economic dimension to servitudes. Three points are worth making. First, the existence of servitude rights leads to efficient use of property. In the case of rural servitudes, land which would otherwise be unusable because it was landlocked by a neighbour's land or because it had no water source of its own could become usable by means of a servitude right of access or of water. In the case of urban servitudes, property for which extraordinary levels of light were required or a building of exceptional height was needed could become usable by means of a servitude right to light or to build.

Second, there was no entitlement to acquire such a right from a neighbour, so it would be necessary for a person who wanted his land to benefit from a servitude right to negotiate for it. This means that everything turned on the relative bargaining positions of the parties. This is a clear illustration of the individualistic stance which Roman law often adopts: you get what you pay for.

Third, because the servitude right affected the property itself in perpetuity it was necessary to develop rules about what could be the legitimate subjects of servitude rights. Clearly, if this was not done, there was a risk that the beneficial economic effects of servitudes would be lost, for instance, if a piece of land became burdened in perpetuity with so many rights in favour of other landowners that the basic content of ownership was reduced virtually to nothing. This is a good reason why there could be no servitude to stroll, pick apples or consume picnics (Paul, *D.* 8.1.8 pr.). Although an economic argument for delimiting the acceptable content of servitudes is not advanced explicitly, it does appear to lie behind some of the criteria which servitudes had to satisfy: they must be for the benefit of the dominant land; and they must be exercised with the least possible inconvenience to the servient land.

3. Protection against nuisance, damage and encroachment

In one of his letters, Seneca writes 'I live over a bath-house. Imagine the assortment of voices, the sound of which is enough to nauseate you.' He goes on to elaborate: the groans and sighs of people exercising; others playing with balls and loudly keeping count of the score; thieves being arrested; great splashes as people jump into the pool; and the cries of sausage sellers and peddlers (*epistulae morales* 56.1–2). So urban life in Rome could be exceptionally unpleasant, and the neighbours exceptionally tiresome. But the protection given against them in Rome was rather limited. This is the more significant given that a large number of people lived in a relatively confined space.

Nowadays many antisocial and tiresome activities of neighbours can be restrained on the ground of nuisance. This is a broad general doctrine, and it is the more effective because it is accepted that the proper approach to the question whether there is a nuisance is from the standpoint of the victim and not the offender; regardless how normal the use the defendant is making of his property, if it exposes the plaintiff to intolerable inconvenience, it can be enjoined (and in some cases damages can be sought).

There is no such general doctrine in Roman law. Instead there was a range of remedies, each of which was specific to a particular situation. For instance, particular interdicts covered infringement of particular servitudes (titles *D.* 43.19, 20 and 22 are examples). There were some more general remedies too. But gaps gaped between these remedies. It is worth looking at the main remedies more closely.

(1) Where a neighbour wrongfully caused physical harm to property, it might be possible to make use of the ordinary action for damages for negligently causing harm (which of course applied in many contexts other than this), the *actio legis Aquiliae*. But this was not altogether straightforward. It was necessary, in the first place, to prove that the defendant had caused the harm, and some jurists took a strict line on this. So, for example, Labeo took the view that if someone piled up earth against his neighbour's wall, the earth was soaked by constant rain, and this caused dampness in and the eventual collapse of the wall, the neighbour was not liable under the *lex Aquilia*, because it was not the neighbour's act (the piling of the earth) but the dampness percolating from the pile which caused the loss (Iavolenus citing Labeo, *D.* 19.2.57).

An even more serious restriction on this remedy was that it was apparently a good defence to the action that the loss resulted from the normal use of property. This seems to be the reason why the jurist Proculus said there was no liability when the heat from a neighbour's oven, which was placed against a common wall, had damaged the wall (Ulpian citing Proculus, *D.* 9.2.27.10).

In short, this remedy depended on showing that the neighbour was at fault, but fault required that he was doing something which was not a normal use of his property. That might not be at all easy; and the problems this might raise seem all the more serious on reflection that Roman housing was not zoned or neatly divided into residential and commercial areas, but baths, bakeries and commercial enterprises (perhaps even cheese factories: see below) might form part of the same building (Wallace-Hadrill 1994: 131–4). There is no reason to doubt that the problem addressed to Proculus was a real problem.

There were however certain remedies which made it possible to prevent a neighbour making even an ordinary or normal use of his property. These were available in highly specific circumstances. Some of the remedies were peculiar to rural use and others to urban.

(2) The 'action for warding off rainwater' (*actio aquae pluviae arcendae*) imposed liability for damage caused by rainwater in very specific circumstances: the defendant had to have built a construction which caused rainwater to harm the plaintiff's land. The rationale of this action was the protection of agricultural land. It was therefore available only for harm done to land, not to buildings; and for the same reason some types of construction did not give rise to liability, notably works built for agricultural purposes. If the defendant lost the action, judgment was given for a sum of money, but the formula in the action was devised so as to encourage the defendant to remove the offending construction rather than pay the money. (More detail on this point is given in chapter 6.)

This action already existed at the time of the Twelve Tables, in the middle of the fifth century BC (Pomponius, *D.* 40.7.21 pr.). Since Roman society at that time was overwhelmingly agricultural, the fact that this action appeared so early is unsurprising. The exception made for constructions built for agricultural purposes also makes good sense, although from when it dates is unclear.

It is remarkable that, although some early jurists such as Trebatius took a broader view, the classical notion of the scope of this action was rather narrow: it was rigidly confined to 'rainwater', so if the complaint was about polluted or hot water, the action was not available (Ulpian citing Trebatius, *D.* 39.3.3 pr.–1). Equally, the action was directed only at 'warding off' water. No action was given to a person whose complaint was that his neighbour had intercepted his water supply, although it might be thought that this was a potentially serious cause of action (Ulpian, *D.* 39.3.1.11–12, 21; Paul, *D.* 39.3.2.9). Only if a servitude right to the water existed would an interdict be available for this sort of infringement (Ulpian, *D.* 43.20.1.7 and 1.19).

It is true that some of the texts just referred to suggest that there might have been a remedy had the neighbour's motive been malicious. But it is doubtful whether this represents classical law. It would anyway be difficult to prove that a neighbour's activities on his own land were so lacking in any possible utility to him that they must have been motivated purely by malice.

(3) An important remedy, probably of greater importance in an urban environment, was known as *damnum infectum*. Gaius defines this as 'loss which has not yet occurred (*nondum factum*) but which we fear will occur' (*D.* 39.2.2). The importance of this remedy was – as the name suggests – that it allowed protection to be sought against the threat of future loss. Again, this protection was available in very specific situations, that is, where a person anticipated suffering loss in the future from a neighbour's building, site or work of construction which was in danger of collapse. The threatened neighbour could seek a promise (*cautio*) from his neighbour that he would indemnify him in the event of loss; and the praetor exercised measures to attempt to compel the giving of the promise.

Although it is not altogether straightforward to reconcile the texts in the Digest, it appears that the provisions for *damnum infectum* were aimed at restricting what would otherwise have been legitimate activities on an owner's own land. For example, a person was wholly at liberty to dig a large hole on his land, even if this intercepted his neighbour's water supply. But he could be compelled under this procedure to give the promise, if it threatened the collapse of his neighbour's wall (Ulpian, *D.* 39.2.24.12 and 26; Paul, *D.* 39.2.25).

The importance of this remedy lay in the fact that there was otherwise no clear entitlement to claim if a building collapsed owing to its owner's failure to maintain it: to make a case under the *lex Aquilia* would be difficult, since there was not normally liability for the consequences of omissions. In short, everything turned on obtaining the promise in advance of the damage (Gaius, *D.* 39.2.6). Even so, liability under the promise would be triggered only if the loss was caused by a fault in the building or construction and not, for instance, by violent storms or by someone's negligence (Ulpian, *D.* 39.2.24.7 and 10).

Although the circumstances in which liability could be brought home to the owner of the moribund property were therefore limited, none the less this device, of inducing its owner to undertake contractual liability for the loss, filled what would otherwise have been a serious gap in the law. For example, the case mentioned above of the wall collapsing owing to the penetration of dampness could have been solved in this way (Alfenus, *D.* 8.5.17.2).

(4) Related to, and sometimes overlapping with, *damnum infectum* was *operis novi nuntiatio*, a term which may be inelegantly translated as the 'denunciation of new work'. This was the remedy where the complainant's concern was that he would suffer harm from new construction which his neighbour was undertaking on his own land. The sort of harm relevant for the purposes of the remedy were such things as encroachment onto or emissions into the complainant's own land, infringement of a servitude, *damnum infectum*, or incompatibility with building regulations (Ulpian, *D.* 39.1.1.16–17; *D.* 39.1.5.8–9). The complainant could serve a notice on the builder to cease work. The builder had then to desist or else give a promise (*cautio*) to destroy the new works if they turned out to be unwarranted (Ulpian, *D.* 39.1.21). If the builder carried on regardless, the complainant was able to seek an order from the praetor, an interdict, to have the work complained of demolished.

Since there might well be urgency about these proceedings, they were extremely informal: the notice was a private notice which had to be served at the place where the building was taking place and must make it clear exactly what construction where was being complained of (Ulpian, *D.* 39.1.5.3–4, 15). At this stage the complainant did not need to demonstrate any right to prohibit the work. That became material only at the later stage if the respondent sought to have the order set aside. In effect, therefore, the serving of the notice made it clear to the builder that, if he persisted in building, he did so at his own risk and might be required to demolish what he had built.

This remedy too therefore offered a neighbour some protection against unwelcome activity taking place on someone else's land. Its scope was somewhat broader than *damnum infectum*, but it was confined to building work which was still under way.

(5) On the other hand, if the building had already been completed, another remedy might still meet the case. This was the general interdict *quod vi aut clam*, named after its opening words ('what by force or stealth. . .'). In essence this forced people to give notice to their neighbours if they intended to build anything which would either encroach onto the neighbouring land or would obstruct the neighbour's use of a

servitude over their own (i.e. the builder's) land. The interpretation given to the terms 'force' and 'stealth' was rather broad: *vis* did not in fact require any force at all but simply that the work should be done contrary to a prohibition, while for something to be done *clam* it was necessary only that it be done without giving notice. The usual reason for not giving notice would of course be that the person notified would object. It was not enough simply to indicate generally that work would be taking place: it was necessary to indicate when, where, and what was to be constructed. If the work was done by force or stealth in these broad senses of the words, then the complainant could obtain this interdict from the praetor ordering the removal of the work.

These proceedings did not go into the question whether the respondent to the interdict might be entitled to do what he had done: the fact that it had been done by force or stealth was sufficient ground for the thing complained of to be removed.

(6) Unusual servitudes. As we have seen, servitudes could be used to adjust neighbours' respective entitlements to light, or to discharge rainwater, and so forth. What is much less clear is whether servitudes were extended to deal with other potential inconveniences of urban life. A well-known text in the Digest deals with the sufferings of those whose houses were near premises on which a particularly noxious smoked cheese was produced.

Aristo gave an opinion to Cerellius Vitalis that he did not think that smoke could lawfully be discharged from a cheese factory into the buildings higher up unless they are subject to a servitude to this effect. He also says that it is not permissible to discharge water or any other substance from the upper onto the lower property, as a man is only allowed to carry out operations on his own premises to the extent that he discharges nothing onto the property of another; and the emission of smoke is just like that of water. The upper proprietor can therefore bring an action against the lower one asserting that he has no right to act in this way. He reports that Alfenus writes that an action can be brought alleging that a man does not have the right to hew stone on his own land in such a way that broken pieces fall onto the plaintiff's land. . . . (Ulpian, *D.* 8.5.8.5)

This is one of very few texts in the Digest suggesting that, by analogy with emission of water, emission of other substances such as smoke or steam might be regulated by servitude. Another text, also setting out the views of an early jurist, suggests that there might be a servitude allowing one person to emit dampness into a neighbour's wall (Alfenus, *D.* 8.5.17.2). But there is no more evidence of this for classical law. If, however, such things could be regulated by servitude, that is clearly significant. Yet there would be no automatic protection against all fumes or any dampness: protection going beyond a normal and reasonable level would have to be be negotiated as a servitude right, and so an unusual sensitivity towards fumes might prove expensive. There is no suggestion in any of the texts that noise could be restrained in any such way.

Some conclusions

The most obvious conclusion is that the law relating to neighbours was extremely complicated. Without legal assistance, it would be quite difficult to know what, if any, remedy was available in any given case. It seems clear enough that neighbours were fairly well protected against the effects of building: three different remedies were potentially useful, depending on where the offending building was being built and whether it was in the course of construction or already completed (*damnum infectum; operis novi nuntiatio;* interdict *quod vi aut clam*). But apart from this, protection was piecemeal and incomplete. Perhaps most striking of all is that in many cases adequate protection will have depended on reaching agreement with the neighbour in advance, either as to the terms of a servitude or by means of the promise on *damnum infectum*. Fortune therefore favoured the neighbour with deep pockets.

CHAPTER 5

Commerce

This chapter deals with the main legal issues which arise in connexion with Roman commerce: contract in general; the main commercial contracts: sale, contracts of loan and for security; contracts for services, such as carriage of goods and building contracts. It then moves on to deal with how Roman businesses may have been organized: what sort of labour they used; and how they attempted to limit their liability. It concludes with the law of insolvency.

I CONTRACTS FORMAL AND INFORMAL

Contracts in Roman law can be divided into two main categories, formal and informal. First, there was the formal contract of *stipulatio*, which was made orally, not in writing. It was concluded by question and answer, which had to be in formal terms and had to correspond with one another. The promisee (or *stipulator*) would ask, for example, 'do you promise to pay 1,000 sesterces?', and the promisor must reply 'I promise to pay 1,000 sesterces.' The exact correspondence between question and answer created an obligation binding on the promisor; but, if the two did not correspond exactly, no obligation came into being. There is much to be said for this insistence on exact correspondence, since it leaves it absolutely clear which verbal exchanges create binding obligations and which do not. The high classical jurists tolerated no discrepancy between question and answer; later this came to be watered down, so that a request for 1,000 sesterces and a promise for 500 sesterces might be held good for the lesser amount, on the basis that the lesser was included within the greater.

So long as there was the necessary formal correspondence of question and answer, there was no restriction on the possible content of the promise – apart from the fact that an illegal or immoral promise would be unenforceable. *Stipulatio* could therefore be used to give legal force to an agreement of any kind. It was a formal contract but an extremely flexible one. It was also a contract *stricti iuris*: its terms were interpreted strictly.

The second type of contract was precisely the opposite: entirely free of form. But each kind was applicable in only one specific situation. Contracts of this sort fall into various sub-categories, but for present purposes it is enough to say that some came into being when an object was delivered (contracts *re*: deposit, loan, pledge) and others came into being by agreement (consensual contracts: sale, hire, mandate, partnership). In neither case was there any need for any set form. But the enforceability of the contract depended on its meeting the precise legal definition for that particular contract. If it did not, there was no contract.

The difference between these two types of contract is fundamental. In the *stipulatio* a promise or series of promises was made, specifically adapted to the contractual situation at which the parties aimed. In consensual contracts, the law already set out the essentials which applied to a contract. So, for example, the consensual contract of sale (*emptio venditio*) included implied warranties on the part of the seller about his title to the goods and about their quality. In a sale by *stipulatio* such matters would need to be provided for expressly if they were to be terms of the contract.

On the other hand, in *mutuum*, the real contract of loan of money (or other measurable commodities), the contract was formed purely by the delivery of the money. But that was in some respects unsatisfactory: the contract of *mutuum* as such made no provision for the date for repayment of the loan; nor did it say anything about the payment of interest. If those were to be terms of the contract, they needed to be introduced by *stipulatio*.

These examples confirm the vital importance of *stipulatio*, both for concluding non-standard contracts and for adding non-standard terms to standard contracts.

In classical law it was therefore characteristic of the law of informal contracts that each contract had its own name; situations which fell outside the recognized categories were simply not contracts. Clearly, this leaves a wide range of cases. The most obvious is perhaps barter: one of the essentials of the contract of sale (as we shall see in the next section) was that the price should be in money. An exchange of goods for goods, barter, was therefore not a sale, and for most of classical law it was not a contract at all. But towards the end of the classical period there are signs of an extension of the law of contract to cover even these anomalous situations, and there is the development of a category of so-called 'innominate' (literally, 'nameless') contracts. These covered arrangements for exchange of goods or services. If we ask why this development took place precisely in the late classical period, we are confronted with a choice familiar from chapter 2: on the one hand, it is arguable that this was a purely technical legal development, a change which the jurists regarded as desirable, having formed the view that the law of contracts had hitherto been too restricted in its scope; on the other hand, it might be thought that this was a reflection of some social change, and that social agreements which had hitherto worked perfectly well on an informal basis now came to be regarded as needing legal recognition and sanction. Which of these is more probable it is, as usual, impossible with any certainty to say.

II SALE

The emergence of the consensual contract of sale (*emptio venditio*) was a critical moment in the history of Roman commerce. Previously sale must have depended on an exchange of *stipulationes*, in which the seller promised to deliver the object of sale, and the buyer promised to pay the price. That had various drawbacks: formality; the fact that routine terms (for example, warranties of quality) had to be spelled out and formally promised in each individual contract; and the fact that the buyer and seller (or their slaves on their behalf) must meet face to face in order to make the contract. The development of the consensual contract of sale – at latest in the second century BC – overcame all of these disadvantages.

The contract of sale came into being only if there was agreement on the essentials: this meant on the object of sale and on the price. This does not sound very demanding. But it did have two important consequences. First, it meant that it was not possible to have a contract of sale with a price to be fixed in the future or (according to some jurists) by reference to a third party, since agreement on a price was interpreted as meaning agreement on a fixed price rather than agreement on how the price was to be arrived at.

Second, it meant that there could be no sale of generic goods, such as a litre of wine or a pound of corn. These cases were not regarded as satisfying the requirement that the object of the contract must be identified. A sale of generic goods was therefore regarded as coming into being only when the actual goods which were to be the subject of the sale had been

identifiably separated from the rest of the goods; or where the whole
stock of goods rather than its individual parts was the object of the sale
(Gaius, *D.* 18.1.35.5–7). The same problem would arise where, for
example, a price per sheep was agreed, but it was not clarified exactly
which sheep from the flock were the subject of the contract. This may
seem more esoteric than practical. If so, the appearance is misleading.
Suppose a second sheep-purchaser came to market and bought the sheep
which the first purchaser thought he had bought, although they had not
been identified. The first could not sue the seller for breach of contract,
because until its object had been identified there was no contract.

These rules about certainty of price and object seem to go back to the
days in which sale was a cash-sale, a transaction in which money and
goods were exchanged on the spot. In developed Roman law, however,
and even in the later republic, there was no need for the buyer and the
seller to perform their parts of the contract at the same time, any more
than this is necessary today. Classical Roman law never broke away from
its refusal to recognize sale of generic goods. This was certainly not
because trade in such goods did not take place: there are plenty of examples of it in the Digest as well as in wrecks at the bottom of the
Mediterranean Sea (cf. Petronius, *Satyricon* 76). The conventional view is
that the law could afford the luxury of this restrictive approach precisely
because the *stipulatio* was still available as a means of entering into a contract for sale of generic goods. Curiously enough, however, there is no
evidence that this approach was followed. Various substitutes for generic
sale could be employed, such as loans repayable in kind, promises to pay
penalties for non-delivery (Paul, *D.* 19.1.47), and so forth; but the lacuna
in the law is perhaps smaller than has generally been appreciated: large
quantities of goods could readily be sold, provided they were identified
at least as a mass, and this would present no problems if they were
housed in a warehouse or on board a ship, while agricultural produce
might often be sold before it was harvested, making its identification
straightforward (Ernst 1996: 276–99, 339–43).

In an ordinary contract of sale (*emptio venditio*) the whole point of the
contract was that without need for express stipulation certain legal
effects were automatically produced. It will be enough to mention three
of these.

(1) The seller impliedly warranted his title to the goods, so that the
buyer who was dispossessed by a person who turned out to be the true
owner was automatically able to sue the seller for breach of contract.
Initially the buyer had to demand a *stipulatio* for indemnity or for a

penalty (conventionally double) in the event that he was evicted from possession of the goods. (A special action was however available as of right if the goods had been made over by the formal conveyance of *mancipatio*.) In due course it became established that as a matter of good faith the seller was obliged to give this promise – so that he could be sued for breach of contract if he did not. The logical conclusion of this development was reached when the guarantee became implicit in the contract of sale itself. This appears to have happened by the early second century AD (Julian, *D*. 21.2.8).

This development illustrates the significance of the fact that sale was a 'good faith' contract. What this meant was that the parties' dealings with one another were assessed in any eventual litigation on the basis of what good faith demanded; and so, without any need for adding further express promises or undertakings, the law on sale kept pace with the customs of trade and commerce: it was open to a judge to find that the failure of a party to act in accordance with ordinary commercial standards was not consonant with good faith and therefore amounted to a breach of contract. The standard of good faith therefore gave the contract extraordinary vitality and flexibility.

(2) The seller impliedly warranted the quality of the goods. Initially the buyer took the risk of defects in the goods: *caveat emptor*. If he wanted a guarantee against particular defects, he would have to take it expressly by *stipulatio*. Only if the seller had fraudulently concealed the presence of defects in the goods would the buyer have a remedy, as this was of course a breach of good faith. In the course of the classical period, however, the aediles – magistrates who were responsible among other things for markets – introduced in their edict a liability for defects which was independent of the seller's knowledge or lack of good faith. The aediles' edict was concerned only with sales of slaves and cattle which took place in the market. (At Athens, the *agoranomoi* performed a similar role: Millett 1990: 172.)

Here we see something of the same pattern as with the warranty against eviction: to start with, the aediles set out a list of defects which the seller should expressly promise were not present; it later became possible to insist that the promise be given; and finally the warranty was implied in the contract. This is essentially the same regime as now governs sales of goods made in the course of business in Britain: the Sale of Goods Act 1979 sets out implied contractual terms on the quality and the fitness for purpose of goods sold. So far as Rome is concerned, the precise chronological steps by which the aediles' liability gradually came to extend to all sales everywhere are uncertain, but the trend was firmly in the direction of a general implied warranty of quality. Where the goods were defective, the buyer was able to reject the goods and reclaim the price within six months or seek a rebate on the price to reflect the presence of the defect within twelve months.

Some of the surviving documents provide an interesting perspective on these warranties. For example, a papyrus of AD 151 attests the sale of a slave who is warranted to be healthy in accordance with the edict; payment of double the price is also promised for the event that the buyer is evicted from possession. Both of these warranties are given by *stipulatio*: particularly interesting is the fact that a reference to the aediles' edict and its list of diseases and defects is incorporated by reference in a *stipulatio*. It is difficult to be sure whether this approach is followed because by this date these warranties were not yet implied in the contract of sale, or whether the buyer was simply reluctant to rely on implied terms and good faith and preferred the certainty of a *stipulatio* (*FIRA* 3.133; cf. also *FIRA* 3.87–9 and 132).

(3) Once agreement had been reached on the essentials of the contract, the object sold and its price, the risk of accidental loss or destruction passed to the buyer. This happened only when the contract was, as the Romans put it, 'perfected', that is, any conditions to which it was subject had been satisfied, and the goods had been identified (where appropriate, by measuring them or weighing them out: Gaius, *D.* 18.1.35.5). It has been regarded as strange that the buyer became liable at such an early point in the transaction, since he would not become owner until the goods were actually conveyed to him, for example by delivery. The result is that, at a time at which he did not own the goods, he was at risk if they were lost or destroyed in certain circumstances. The explanation for this again seems to lie in the fact that sale was originally cash-sale, and conclusion of contract, conveyance and transfer of risk all took place at the same time. That would not account for the survival of the rule at a time when the contract was regularly concluded well before the conveyance of the goods was made. But the risk which passed to the buyer was only for events which were not preventable by the seller, and this restriction was interpreted strictly: the seller was still liable if the goods were stolen, unless the theft involved overwhelming force. So the sorts of risks which the buyer assumed on conclusion of the contract were for destruction by earthquake, flooding or fire (so long as the seller was not responsible for it). The risk rule, odd though it may seem, was therefore kept within strict limits.

The terms just discussed were (ultimately) implied in every contract of sale. But it was possible to introduce further terms ('pacts') into the contract. This could be done without need for additional *stipulatio*, because sale was a 'good faith' contract. One aspect of this was that, where the parties had entered into pacts in conjunction with the sale, the tenor of those pacts should be observed.

Some of these pacts were in the interest of the seller, and others in the interest of the buyer. So, for example, the parties could include in the contract a term allowing the seller to call off the sale if the price was not paid by a certain day or if he received a better offer within a certain period. There were difficulties of interpretation in both of these cases: was the sale concluded immediately but subject to cancellation in the future? Or did it not come into being at all until the price was paid or no better offer was received? The Digest discusses the legal consequences of this choice (Paul, *D.* 41.4.2.3–4; Ulpian, *D.* 18.2.2 and *D.* 18.3.1).

Clearly in the buyer's interest, on the other hand, were arrangements for sale on approval (*pactum displicentiae*) or for tasting of wine before purchase, which appears to have been absolutely standard practice. An interesting example of sale on approval is given by Ulpian; as appears from the end of the text, the buyer seems to have been an acrobat who specialized in jumping from mule to mule (*desultor*):

This question is raised by Mela: if I have given you mules to try out, for you to buy them if you approve them, and for you to pay a daily rental for each one if you do not approve them, and within the trial period the mules have been stolen by thieves, what has to be paid: is it the price and the rental or only the rental? Mela says it makes a difference whether the sale has already been concluded or is to be concluded in the future: if it had already been concluded, the price could be claimed; if it was a future sale the rental could be. He said nothing about the appropriate actions. But I think, if the sale was concluded, the seller would have the action on sale (*actio ex vendito*), and, if not, the appropriate action ought to be given against the acrobat. (Ulpian, *D.* 19.5.20.1)

Here again we find the same concern whether the sale comes into being at once, but is liable to be set aside, or whether it is suspended until the buyer has given his approval. The reason it matters is that the risk of loss of the goods passes to the buyer when the contract is concluded: if the contract has been concluded, the loss falls on the buyer and the seller is entitled to payment of the price.

It seems likely that inclusion of any of these terms in a contract would have affected the price of the goods; and it is clear from the way some jurists discuss them that they were regarded in a sense as being part of the price. Certainly, a buyer who is given generous terms for rejection of goods may have to pay a relatively high price; a seller who insists on stern provisions for calling off the sale may have to make do with a low one. All this gives a clear impression of the way in which the parties could negotiate the terms for their particular contract, using but modifying the basic background of the law of sale.

III LENDING AND BORROWING

1. Loans

Loans could be arranged in a number of different ways. One was of course *stipulatio*: the promisor simply promised to pay a certain sum at a certain date, and this could be calculated so as to include a charge for interest.

There was, however, no need for a *stipulatio*. Simply handing over money as a loan created an obligation on the part of the recipient to repay it. This was the contract known as *mutuum*. The contract came into being, as the Romans put it, *re*, by the very fact of delivery of the money. The obligation to repay was of precisely the same extent. Such a loan accordingly did not include any provision for interest. For this reason, it seems likely that *mutuum* was one of the range of contracts which were employed primarily between friends. Friendship evidently imposed such duties (Cic., *ad familiares* 14.1.5, 14.2.3). Indeed, a good deal of the borrowing in Rome seems to have taken place, just as it did in Athens (Millett 1983: 47; 1991: 218), between friends and relatives, and much of it would be purely for the domestic purposes of consumption or meeting problems of liquidity, rather than for investment. So a loan, although a contract, was not necessarily a commercial transaction: instead it fitted into an elaborate network of obligations owed by one friend to another. Some of these would be ultimately repaid only by a bequest (chapter 3 above; Garnsey and Saller 1987: 154–6).

Whenever the *mutuum* was employed in more commercial dealings, in which interest would have been demanded, it would have been necessary to enter into a separate contract for the interest. That could have been done by *stipulatio*; on the other hand, if a *stipulatio* had to be made for the interest anyway, it is not unlikely that it would have been extended to cover the principal too. In effect, therefore, the *mutuum* would be superseded (in legal language, 'novated') by the contract of *stipulatio*.

Maximum interest rates were legally fixed from time to time. The history and the details are rather obscure, although it is tolerably clear that throughout the classical period the maximum rate was the so-called *centesimae usurae*, 1 per cent per month, and so 12 per cent per year (Zimmermann 1990: 166–70).

The documents of practice illustrate a variety of approaches to loans; although it is important to note that very similar examples are also found in the Digest (Paul, *D.* 12.1.40 and *D.* 45.1.126.2), so theory and practice here go hand in hand. Here is one of the Murecine tablets:

[29 August AD 38] I, C. Novius Eunus, have written that I owe Hesychus Evenianus, the slave of C. Caesar Augustus Germanicus, 1130 sesterces which I received from him as a loan (*mutuum*) and shall repay either to him or to C. Sulpicius Faustus, as soon as he demands them. And Hesychus Evenianus, the slave of C. Caesar Augustus Germanicus, stipulated and I, C. Novius Eunus, promised that the 1130 sesterces above mentioned were duly paid in good coin. Transacted at Puteoli. (TP 17)

Here the loan is a *mutuum*, but it appears to have been reinforced by a *stipulatio*. This raised a legal question: did a *mutuum* come into being at all, or was the whole transaction just a *stipulatio*? Or did the *stipulatio* novate an existing *mutuum*? Or did both subsist concurrently? The later classical jurists appear to have favoured the view that it was just a *stipulatio* (Pomponius, *D.* 46.2.7; Ulpian, *D.* 46.2.6.1). In the case of this document, however, there is some reason to believe that both transactions were regarded as subsisting, so that the creditor would have a choice which type of action to pursue (Wolf and Crook 1989: 22).

There is an interesting development in the following year, in which another document (TP 18) attests a loan transaction between the same parties, this time for 1,250 sesterces, again reinforced by a *stipulatio*, but this time also by an oath to repay the principal sum on or before 1 November. Failure to repay not only brings with it the sanction of perjury but also a penalty of twenty sesterces per day for late payment. From this one can safely conclude that this particular lender was tiring of this particular borrower. The general conclusion, however, must be that parties had a broad freedom to fix the terms of their own contracts. A puzzle about this and other similar documents which has yet satisfactorily to be explained is that, viewed as a rate of interest, the penalty is considerably in excess of any legal rate.

2. Bankers

An interesting feature of the tablet just cited (TP 17) is that it mentions
C. Sulpicius Faustus as an alternative payee to whom repayment of the
loan could be made. He was the banker in whose archive this tablet was
found, together with a large number of other documents of loan and
security and other matters (some of which are discussed below). These
tablets confirm that, although Rome had no banking system as such, and
much credit and lending appears to have taken place on the basis of personal rather than commercial relationships, there were none the less
bankers in the sense of people who accepted deposits, on which they
might pay interest, who acted as paying agents, and who lent out money
against interest. The leading study of Roman banking concludes that
bankers tended to operate at a local level (Andreau 1987: 652); this finds
some support in the case of the Sulpicii, who appear to have been a
banking 'house' at Puteoli: three generations of them are attested, all
apparently freedmen.

So far as loans made by bankers are concerned, only a little need be
added here to what has been said already. Comparison of the two documents just mentioned indicates that, as would be expected, bankers
varied the stringency of the terms of their loans, presumably taking
account of the attractiveness of retaining the particular customer.

It is interesting that the document cited above (TP 17) requires repayment of the loan on demand. This is not an unworkable provision
(modern overdrafts are also repayable on demand), but it can only have
worked if desirable customers at least were given notice when repayment of their loan would be demanded. It is very striking that none
of the documents in this archive, or the similar documents from
Herculaneum, contains any date for repayment of the loan. Nor do they
make any provision for payment of interest. Since altruism and banking
do not go hand in hand, some explanation is needed. Because the documents specify no definite term for the loan, it is impossible to conclude
that the capital sum already included an advance reckoning of the
amount of interest due. There is also no evidence of separate documents
which might have contained agreements on interest. A strong possibility
is therefore that payment of interest was provided for informally, in a
pact. That would not allow the creditor to sue for it, but his position may
have been sufficiently protected by the fact that the loan was repayable
on demand; if the debtor was not paying the interest, one can be fairly
sure that repayment would soon be demanded. It may also be that this

method allowed the creditor to avoid the restrictions on interest rates which would otherwise have applied (Paul, *D.* 2.14.4.3; Gröschler 1997: 149–94, 371–2 on TP Sulp 60–2 and TH 70–4).

So far as bankers' borrowing money or taking deposits is concerned, clearly a loan (*mutuum*) could be made to a banker as to any other individual. A more interesting possibility, however, was to make not a loan but a deposit (*depositum*). Under the ordinary contract of deposit, the depositee was not entitled to use the object deposited and to do so was a breach of contract. This form of deposit would therefore be of interest to bankers only for safe deposits or where the money was not going to be touched at all. In general, however, bankers will have wished to make use of the money and return not the precise coins deposited but the equivalent value. This could be done either by *mutuum* or by so-called 'irregular deposit', a type of deposit in which the depositee was able to use the object deposited.

The details of this arrangement are extremely controversial. What is at least clear is that it was imported from Hellenistic practice and eventually acclimatized in Rome. At least in late classical law it appears to have been accepted – although still not without dispute – that, where the depositee (the banker) used the money, he came under an obligation to pay interest: the jurists could deduce this consequence from the fact that deposit was a good faith contract (Scaevola, *D.* 16.3.28: Papinian, *D.* 16.3.24). The Digest contains evidence of deposits where the money was not to be touched and those where it was, as well as deposits where interest was to be paid and those where it was not (Ulpian, *D.* 42.5.24.2 and *D.* 16.3.7.2). The difference between these types emerged most clearly if the bank failed: those whose money had not been touched and who could identify it as theirs could simply claim their property back; those whose money had been used but who had not received interest had a preferential claim in the insolvency; whereas those who had received interest ranked together with ordinary creditors of the banker (Andreau 1987: 529–44; Bürge 1987: 552–8; Zimmermann 1990: 215–19; Kaser 1971: 536).

This evidence seems to suggest that there was a range of possibilities open to a Roman who had cash to spare, and which option he chose would depend on what risk he was prepared to accept (cf. perhaps Plin., *ep.* 10.54–5). Or, viewed from the other perspective, it seems likely (just as is the case today) that bankers with less good credit ratings would have to offer better interest rates in order to encourage customers to deposit with them.

3. Investment and securities

All the evidence points to land constituting the main and most important element in wealth in Roman times. The ancient sources depict it as
being a safe investment, but suggest that anything else was more fragile
and might be fraught with great risk (Plin., *ep.* 3.19.8; Kehoe 1997: 76,
135). None the less, the economy was not purely agricultural. When
Pliny found a surplus of municipal funds his first reaction was to attempt
to buy land with it; when there was none to be had, he attempted to
arrange to lend out the money (Plin., *ep.* 10.54–5). Those with free wealth
did invest in businesses: Caesar, for example, had shares in a tax-farming
enterprise; and Cato in a shipping business (Cic., *in Vatinium* 29; Plutarch,
Cato maior 21.6–7). It is likely too that some of their investments will have
been in the shape of personal debts. This raises the issue of credit and
forms of security. Modern businesses depend on ready access to credit
and are vitally affected by the means of borrowing available to them and
the types of security with which they are able to secure their indebtedness. It is not self-evident that similar considerations apply to pre-
industrial societies such as that of ancient Rome. None the less,
capital-intensive businesses such as shipping must have called for borrowing, and sometimes that borrowing will have had to be secured.

Two main categories of security have to be considered: personal security, in which another person guarantees that the debtor will pay; and real
security, in which property is pledged to the creditor to guarantee
payment. Nowadays, although personal security is by no means extinct
(loans to private companies are regularly secured by personal guarantees
granted by their directors), real security is the commoner form, most typically in the form of a mortgage secured against land. A critical
difference between Rome and the modern world is that the Romans had
a marked preference for personal rather than real security. It is quite possible that there is a question of status involved here: a wealthy Roman's
word was his bond, and security as potent as any pledge. The same may
not of course have been true at the lower levels of the social scale.

4. Personal security

There were three main types of personal security, *sponsio*, *fidepromissio* and
fideiussio, which differ in a number of more or less technical respects. The
details are avoided here, and what follows is very much a broad-brush
picture. All three types of security were founded on a *stipulatio*, in which

the promisor or surety undertook an obligation towards the creditor, just as the principal debtor had done. The obligation might be for the same amount as the debtor's liability or it might be for less, but it could not be for more. How easy it was to find someone to undertake this obligation would of course vary from case to case, but there is little doubt that undertaking personal security was part of the code of (mainly upper-class) social duty which was based on friendship and good faith. As Fritz Schulz said, 'Roman friends made mutual claims on each other which would in many cases cause a modern "friend" to break off the friendship without delay' (Schulz 1936: 233; Konstan 1997: 80).

The two obligations, of the principal and the surety, were interrelated: each was regarded as being an obligation for the same thing (*eadem res*). The most important practical consequence of this was that, because it was not possible to sue for the same thing twice, when the creditor sued either the principal debtor or the surety, the other was automatically released from liability. This meant that it was important to choose correctly whom to sue; although it appears to have been regarded as improper to sue the surety without first calling on the principal to repay (Cic., *Att.* 16.15.2; Gaius, *D.* 47.10.19). But the basic conception of Roman suretyship which this reveals was that the whole of the debt should be recovered from one person. In order to maximize the chances of being able to do this, the creditor had an interest in maximizing the number of sureties, in the hope that at least one would be solvent at the time the debt fell due.

Another form of personal suretyship is also attested, which proceeds upon a different basis: here the surety undertook only to indemnify the creditor against the amount he was unable to recover from the principal debtor. Obviously, in this instance the creditor had to proceed first against the principal. But since in this case the obligation undertaken by the surety was not the same as that of the principal debtor, the action against the principal debtor would not extinguish it (Celsus, *D.* 12.1.42 pr.).

Once the surety paid the creditor, he in effect acquired the creditor's own claim against the debtor. It is not possible to go into the details here; in essence, however, the surety was treated as having been given a mandate by the principal debtor to become his surety. Once he had performed the mandate, in accordance with general principles he was entitled to reimbursement (Gaius, *Inst.* 3.127).

Personal security was evidently of the greatest importance. That is clear not just from the steady refinement of the rules, tending to increase its practical utility, but also from the extraordinary volume of legislation which dealt with it. For the details we are indebted to one of Gaius's historical excursuses, in which he lists no fewer than five republican statutes which altered the rules on personal security (*Inst.* 3.121–7). Their dates are not entirely clear. A *lex Publilia* gave the surety an action against the principal debtor if he was not reimbursed within six months; a *lex Apuleia* (after 241 BC?) ruled that one of several sureties who had paid off the creditor in full could recover part of his payment from the other sureties; a *lex Furia* (before 81 BC) limited the liability of each of several sureties to a proportionate share of the whole debt, and also released them after two years; a *lex Cicereia* required a debtor to declare the amount of the debt and the number of sureties and, if he failed to do so, released the sureties; and a *lex Cornelia* (81 BC) limited the amount for which one could in any given year stand surety for any given individual to 20,000 sesterces. The obvious conclusion from all this legislative activity is that there was great concern to relieve the position of the surety.

Legislation continued under the empire. A ruling of Hadrian reaffirmed that if a surety could prove that there were other solvent sureties, the creditor had to restrict his claim against him to his proportionate share.

5. Real security

Real security in Roman law can be divided into three types.

(1) The first, *fiducia*, was a form of security in which the debtor transferred ownership of some property to the creditor. The creditor undertook to reconvey the property to the debtor when the debt was repaid. The creditor was full owner of the thing for the time being, but his ownership was qualified by the terms of his undertaking (or *fiducia*): on repayment he must reconvey the property; meantime he had to look after it, he could not (yet) sell it, and he had to offset profits made through the thing against the debt owed. A fairly complete example of such a transaction is preserved in a tablet from Spain dating from the first or second century AD (*FIRA* 3.92).

But this undertaking was a purely personal one in favour of the debtor, and the debtor's rights against the creditor were therefore only *in personam*: that is, they were good only to enforce this personal agreement. If the creditor breached the *fiducia* and conveyed the property to a third party, the debtor had no right to recover it, since he was not the owner. This seems to be true even if the third party knew of the existence of the *fiducia*.

It will be obvious that this form of security placed the creditor in a very strong position – as owner of the security – and the debtor in a correspondingly weak one. Whether any given transaction made use of *fiducia* will therefore have depended to some extent on the bargaining strengths of the respective parties. But there would be other relevant considerations too. Since *fiducia* made the creditor owner, there was no need for him to retain possession of the secured property; he would anyway be able to recover it from a person in possession of it by using the owner's action for recovery of property (*vindicatio*). This is important, since it meant that the creditor could let the debtor continue to use the property, either informally or under a rental agreement, and would not thereby jeopardize his security. And the advantage to the debtor was that he could pledge even property which he needed in order to generate income to repay the debt. (As we shall see, this was not true of another form of real security, *pignus*.)

The advantages and disadvantages of *fiducia* are therefore more finely balanced than at first appears. Although *fiducia* was abolished by Justinian, and therefore does not appear in the Digest, a good deal of documentary evidence survives indicating that it was used throughout the classical period.

(2) *Pignus* was a form of security in which the debtor remained owner of the property he was pledging, and what he transferred to the creditor was possession. From the point of view of the debtor this was an improvement in one respect, since if the creditor parted with the property, the debtor, being owner, was able to recover it. But it suffered from the drawback that, since the creditor was in possession, the debtor would be deprived of the use of his property. That was a critical restriction on what he could pledge, since any property he depended on to cultivate his land or to operate his business could not be used as security. It follows that he was in effect limited to pledging property which was surplus to his requirements. Even the creditor could not use the pledged property unless this was agreed; if he drew income or fruits from it, these had to be set off against the interest payable on the loan, failing which the capital.

To overcome this inconvenience, the law seems to have developed so as to allow pledges to be made, for example, of a tenant's basic agricultural equipment, without his having to give up possession (Labeo, *D.* 20.6.14). This seems, however, to have required express agreement; by contrast, in an urban tenancy the tenant's belongings were impliedly pledged against payment of the rent (Neratius, *D*. 20.2.4). Further examples of pledges without possession are discussed below in connexion with hypothec.

On default by the debtor, the creditor had two remedies. First, an interdict to recover possession of the pledged goods from the debtor or anyone else who had them; this was known as the *interdictum Salvianum* (Gaius, *Inst*. 4.147). Clearly this would be needed only if the pledge creditor lost the possession which he was initially given. Second, the creditor had an action to recover the property if it had been disposed of to a third party. The dates at which these remedies were developed are unclear, but it may be that they go back to the first century BC (Kaser 1971: 472–3).

(3) Under a third, evidently later, form of security, hypothec, the creditor obtained neither ownership nor possession but had only the right to take possession when the debt fell due, if it was not then paid. The same remedies were available to the creditor under this form of security; the difference was of course that the creditor would need to use one of them to obtain possession in the first place.

Hypothec offered the clear advantage to the debtor that he could realize the equity value of things – including land, with which there is some reason to associate this form of security – while he continued to use them to earn his living and to repay his indebtedness. Indeed, since the debtor did not have to surrender any specific property, it was possible to interpret a hypothec as creating a security right over goods the debtor would acquire in the future. This could clearly be of the greatest value for businesses, which turned over their stock on a regular basis. Here is an example:

A debtor pledged a stall (*taberna*) to his creditor. It was asked whether this was a nullity or whether he was to be regarded as having pledged, under the term *taberna*, the goods which were in it. And if, over the course of time, he had sold those goods and had bought others and brought them into the *taberna*, and he had then died, would the creditor be able with his action (*actio hypothecaria*) to claim all the goods found there, even if the types of goods had changed and different ones brought in? He replied: the goods which were in the debtor's *taberna* at the time of his death are regarded as being subject to the pledge. (Scaevola, *D*. 20.1.34 pr.)

The fact that the debtor did not need to surrender ownership or possession of the security had one other major consequence: he was able to offer the same property as security more than once. The principle is the same as in a modern mortgage of land: a borrower who has already borrowed against the value of his land is able to take out further loans, provided there remains equity in the land against which creditors are prepared to lend. Plainly this introduces a complication which the other forms of real security do not involve: it becomes necessary to be able to find out how much equity is left in the property offered for security, and to regulate the priority of the various secured creditors. The second point seems to have caused some analytical difficulty for a while; the earliest cases suggest that the validity of the second security was treated as being conditional on the discharge of the first, so that there was an insistence that only one pledge could be valid at a time (Africanus, *D.* 20.4.9.3). But this view was gradually overcome, and a second pledge which was valid independently of the first was recognized by the mid-to-late second century AD (Marcellus, *D.* 20.4.12.7; Paul, *D.* 44.2.30.1; Ulpian, *D.* 20.1.10). Once this stage was reached, it became established that an earlier creditor took priority over a later (*prior tempore potior iure*: *C.* 8.17.3 (AD 213)), and that a later creditor, by paying off an earlier one, could succeed to his place in the security ranking.

Much more problematic was the first point: knowledge of the existence or extent of prior charges. That is regulated nowadays at least for charges on land or company charges by a register of charges: the existence of such a register makes it possible to say that a creditor knew (or ought to have known) of the existence of prior charges against the secured property. But the creation of such registers for movable property is plainly difficult, now as in Rome. The closest to this sort of solution that we seem to find in Rome is a constitution of the emperor Leo in AD 472, which provided that pledges which were publicly documented should take priority over those that were not, even if they had been established earlier (*C.* 8.17.11). During the classical period, however, there does not seem to have been any adequate means of addressing this problem. Attempts to compel full disclosure seem to have been half-hearted. For example, it was made a crime for a debtor to mislead a creditor as to the extent of existing borrowing against a property which he was offering as security (*C.* 9.34.1 (AD 231); *C.* 9.34.4 (AD 244)). The offence fell under the generic heading of fraud, *stellionatus*, literally 'behaving like a gecko'. Geckos have not so far been confirmed as tending to act in this way. But, just as the debtor leaves the creditor empty-handed, so the gecko escapes by shedding its tail in its predator's hands or jaws, leaving him cheated of his main prize (Stein 1990: 82–3).

In classical law it is difficult to see how a creditor could have had much confidence that any property which was still in a debtor's possession was not subject to a prior charge. Nor would this be a problem only for hypothec, since any prior charge would also be good against a subsequently created *fiducia* or *pignus*. Matters can only have been made worse by the tendency in later classical law to subject property to implied or tacit hypothecs for worthy causes (such as the hypothec of a child over property bought by his tutor in his own name but with the child's money; or the hypothec of the fisc for taxes and certain other claims; see Kaser 1971: 466). For all these reasons, it is not clear that classical law ever came to an adequate solution of this problem. The result is that a potentially powerful instrument remained blunt, and the law of real security less useful and versatile than it might have been.

Some documents of practice are interesting on the subject of the various types of security. One recounts, much along the lines of the tablet (TP 17) cited earlier, the making of a loan by Evenius Primianus through his slave Hesychus to C. Novius Eunus, repayable on demand. It continues:

And for these 10000 sesterces I have given him a pledge [*pignus* or *arrabo*] of approximately 7000 modii of Alexandrine wheat and 4000 modii of chickpeas, spelt, monocopi and lentils in 200 sacks. All this I have stored in my possession in the Bassian public stores of Puteoli. I declare that I bear the risk. (TP 15, 28 June AD 37)

From this it is clear that C. Novius Eunus pledged his goods without giving up their possession: this was therefore a case of hypothec. It is worth noting in passing that the value of the pledge greatly exceeded that of the loan: at a conservative valuation of 3 sesterces per modius, the wheat alone was worth 21,000 sesterces (Duncan-Jones 1982: 145–6; on *arrabo*, Millett 1990: 175–6).

Four days later C. Novius Eunus borrowed a further 3,000 sesterces and evidently did give up possession in favour of the creditor: this we can tell not just from the absence in the second document of any reference to his retaining possession but (much more emphatically) from the fact that on the same day the creditor entered into an agreement to rent the part of the public store which held the pledged goods (TP 7 and 16, both 2 July AD 37; Wolf and Crook 1989: 17–20). It is interesting to note that no additional security was taken for the second loan: there was still sufficient equity remaining in the initial security to cover the second advance to the borrower. We seem here to have a picture of increasing desperation on the part of C. Novius Eunus, or of increasing harshness on the part of his creditor: not only is the value of the security demanded very high in relation to the sum advanced, but security with possession is almost immediately taken.

It is time to sum up on securities. The extraordinary concern with regulating the details of personal security suggests that it was regarded as particularly important. Probably those with landed wealth but temporary problems of liquidity would have found little difficulty in arranging for personal guarantors and so managed to secure loans without much personal inconvenience. But it does not seem likely that this would be true very far down the scale of status or wealth. At that point real security is likely to have played a much more vital role.

In the area of real security, on the one hand, there is a good deal of flexibility in the development of different forms of security, so that what the creditor received might be ownership or possession or simply the right to take possession. But, on the other hand, there remained problems: an ordinary *pignus* cannot have been useful for the debtor who needed to retain possession of income-generating property, although concessions were admittedly made to overcome this difficulty. Hypothec, although much more versatile, was much weakened by uncertainty about the extent of prior charges, and in later classical law by a multiplicity of implied hypothecs.

Owing to these inadequacies in the law of real security, small, undercapitalized landowners may have had difficulty in raising cash against the value of their land except by entering into *fiducia*. But security of that sort involved transferring title to the creditor. Probably it was not uncommon for the debtor to continue to farm the land as the tenant of his creditor. Some tenants would find it difficult to redeem the *fiducia*. It is at least possible that in this way the law of real security contributed to the decline of the class of small owner-farmers and the rise of great tenanted estates (Schulz 1951: 403–5; cf. de Neeve 1984: 156).

6. Sea loans and insurance

A special kind of loan was the sea loan (*fenus nauticum* or *pecunia traiecticia*; Millett 1983; de Sainte Croix 1974), which appears to have originated in Hellenistic practice. Here the borrower negotiated a loan from the creditor in order to finance a voyage and the purchase of goods. The characteristic feature of these loans was that if the ship foundered there was no obligation to repay the loan. On the other hand, if the ship returned safely, the loan had to be repaid at a substantial rate of interest. In effect, the sum payable in interest covered not just conventional interest but an insurance premium; for that reason these loans were not subject to the normal rules on maximum interest rates. It seems that dealing of this sort fell outside the ordinary scope of banking practice, although bankers might act as paying agents for the creditors (Andreau 1987: 603–4). Similarly, in Greek practice it seems that there were professional moneylenders who specialized in such loans (Millett 1983: 51; 1991: 188–96).

A well-known example is cited in the Digest. The main terms were these: Stichus, on behalf of his owner, lent money to Callimachus in Beirut; Callimachus was to buy goods with the money and ship them to Brindisi; there he was to sell the goods, buy new goods and ship them back to Beirut; on both legs of the voyage the goods were at his risk; he was also liable to maintain any slave of the lender's who travelled on the voyage with him. The loan was made for a period of 200 days, during which the journey there and back must be completed; the return journey was to begin on or before the ides of September (13 September); if it did not do so, the whole of the loan and interest would fall due as if the voyage had been completed (Scaevola, *D.* 45.1.122.1). These terms were set out in a *stipulatio*.

Winter sailing was extremely hazardous, and the borrower had to be encouraged to complete the voyage well before the weather deteriorated. That is the reason why, in effect, the risk of the venture was placed entirely on the borrower, Callimachus, if he did not embark on the return journey before 13 September. In the event the goods were loaded in time, but the return journey was not commenced until after 13 September. The ship sank. Callimachus was liable.

IV CONTRACTS OF SERVICE

From a vast range of possibilities, there is space only to glance at two types of contract, contracts for carriage of goods or persons, and building contracts.

1. Contracts for carriage

Carriage of goods would generally be governed by the contract of hire (*locatio conductio*). But there was more than one way in which the parties could construct their contractual relationship, and which way they chose will no doubt have depended not just on the particular result they aimed at but also on their relative bargaining positions. For example, they might enter into a contract purely for hire of the ship itself. A contract in this form would not go into the question of delivery of goods at any particular destination; so the rent would be due regardless whether the goods were delivered (Scaevola, *D.* 19.2.61.1).

On the other hand, a proper construction of the contract might indicate that its object was the transporting of particular goods or persons from one place to another. An example of this sort is found in a papyrus of AD 236, in which the master of a ship agrees to transport 250 *artabae* of pulses to Oxyrhynchus for a rental of 100 silver drachmae, 40 payable at once and 60 on delivery. The contract allows time for loading and four days for unloading at Oxyrhynchus, but if the ship is still occupied after that there is an additional charge of 16 drachmae per day (*FIRA* 3.155). In this sort of case, if the delivery did not arrive at the contracted destination, it is likely that no payment would be due (Ulpian, *D.* 19.2.15.6). But the result might be different, depending on the terms of the contract: so, for example, the jurists Labeo and Paul disagree on whether the master of a ship who has contracted to transport cattle is entitled to payment for one which died *en route*. Labeo says no; Paul says it depends on whether payment was agreed for each cow embarked or disembarked (*D.* 14.2.10 pr.). Ulpian raises the question whether a fare is due for a baby born in the course of the voyage. He thinks not, essentially on the basis that a baby does not take up much space and will not be making full use of the facilities on board (*D.* 19.2.19.7). The reasoning does not have much of a legal flavour to it (might one not have said that the contract was to pay a fare for each person who embarked?), although the result accords with common sense.

The carriage of goods by sea was risky; from time to time it was necessary to jettison cargo in order to save a foundering ship. This might work harshly if the ship was saved but the loss of the cargo simply lay where it fell, on the owner of the particular jettisoned cargo. The Romans therefore, like other Mediterranean nations, adopted the rule of the *lex Rhodia* to distribute losses equally among all the cargo owners. This result was reached by making use of the ordinary contractual actions: so those whose goods had been lost would sue the master of the ship for breach of contract (*actio locati*), while those whose goods had been preserved would be liable to be sued by him for a contribution or (more simply) their goods would not be released until they had contributed (Paul, *D.* 14.2.2 pr.). The application of the rule of the *lex Rhodia* gave rise to a number of intriguing problems: was damage to the ship to be treated on an equal footing with damage to cargo? No – this loss falls on the master of the ship. Were those whose cargo – for example, pearls – in effect added no weight also liable to contribute? Yes. If so, in what proportion? According to the value of their goods. Should account be taken of passengers? No – no valuation can be made of free persons (Paul, *D.* 14.2.2.1–2).

2. Building contracts

Building contracts are interesting because they present some of the problems of other contracts writ large: they may involve substantial sums of money; they are relatively long-term; they are complex; and the buildings are meant to last (as indeed some of the Roman ones actually did). These features raise peculiarities about design, terms for payment, risk, and warranties for defects. All of these problems are familiar enough in modern practice.

The Roman sources indicate that building contracts were entered into both by means of *stipulatio* and also by means of the contract of hire (*locatio conductio*): in this case the employer (*locator*) let out the job of construction to the contractor (*conductor*). Although no detailed examples of the *stipulatio* form of a building contract appear to survive, it would be possible (as we have seen in other contexts) for a detailed document to be confirmed by *stipulatio* (Proculus, *D.* 45.1.113 pr.; Papinian, *D.* 45.1.124). The contract would normally at least provide for a completion date, failing which a reasonable time would be understood (Labeo, *D.* 19.2.58.1), and for the specifications to which the building was to be built. A clear surviving documentary example of a building specification is the public works contract to build a wall at Puteoli: there great detail is given about what materials and measurements are to be used (*FIRA* 3.153 of 105 BC; cf. Cato, *de agricultura* 14–15; Labeo, *D.* 19.2.60.3; Martin 1989).

Roman building contracts fell into two categories still commonly in use today: lump sum and measured work. In the first case, the builder is entitled to a lump sum for completing the project, although part of this is typically paid in advance. In the second case, the builder is entitled to payment for the work he has actually done, as measured (Florentinus, *D.* 19.2.36). In the case of measured work, the risk would pass to the employer as he approved each stage (cf. Iavolenus, *D.* 19.2.51.1). The risk of 'acts of God' such as earthquakes would in any event be on the employer, unless otherwise agreed (Florentinus, *D.* 19.2.36; Iavolenus, *D.* 19.2.59).

The critical moment in the contract was when the building was completed and had to be approved by the employer. At least in later law, the standard of approval seems not to have been purely subjective but to have been that of a 'reasonable man' (*bonus vir*: Paul, *D.* 19.2.24 pr.). Approval of the building meant that final payment was due, as well as that the risk now lay wholly on the employer. In particular, it meant that if defects later emerged in the building they were the responsibility of the employer: in modern terms, there was no defects liability period after final approval had been given, unless approval had only been given because the contractor had fraudulently concealed defects in the work (Paul, *D.* 19.2.24 pr.). It would, of course, be possible to contract for a more extensive defects liability.

V THE ORGANIZATION OF BUSINESSES

This section sets out the basic legal rules on agency and liability and then ventures to suggest how, optimally, the Romans might have chosen to organize their business activities to take advantage of the background of these legal rules. Since much of the evidence is drawn from the legal sources, the argument is to some extent inferential and has to be read subject to the methodological caveats mentioned in chapter 2. But since commercial law has to be seen against a background of risk, it seems reasonable to suppose that people would try to reduce their exposure to risk where possible, consistent with taking advantage of opportunities to make profits. There is another reason why they should have taken particular care to do so: procedure in the event of bankruptcy was very harsh. That is discussed in section VI of this chapter.

1. Representation and agency

Although the Roman jurists developed a number of informal contracts such as sale, any contract which was in any way unusual or untypical would have to be entered into by *stipulatio*. That in turn required the presence of the contracting parties face to face. Communications being slow, there was a real restriction on how many contracts any individual could enter into in how many geographically dispersed locations; this strictly limited number was the necessary consequence of the fact that there was a strictly limited number of places in which a person could be at the same time. Accordingly, it became necessary to develop rules for representation, to allow the acts of one person to bind another. This was a breach with the strict principle of Roman law that obligations were personally binding only, and a contract gave rights only to the parties to it and to nobody else.

That rule did not apply, however, where one of the contracting parties was a slave or a child in the paternal power of his father. But that case raised its own difficulties: initially, the paterfamilias could scarcely make use of members of his own family for business purposes, since nobody could usefully be sued for what they did: the paterfamilias was not liable under their contracts (Gaius, *D.* 50.17.133); while slaves had no standing to appear as litigants in court and no proprietary capacity; and dependent children, although they could be sued, had no proprietary capacity and would therefore be unable to satisfy any judgment. So long as this remained the case, clearly nobody would knowingly deal with a slave or dependent child.

All this changed with the development of legal remedies based on the *peculium*. The *peculium* was a fund of property granted by a paterfamilias to a person in his power, whether slave or free. It might be made up of any property: land, movables, businesses, other slaves. It remained the property of the paterfamilias and could be revoked by him, but in practice the person in power had charge of it and could deal with it as if it were his own. There will be more to say about it in connexion with limitation of liability; for the present it is enough to note that the *peculium* allowed slaves and children to make themselves useful, since creditors were now accorded a right of action against the paterfamilias, albeit one restricted to the value of the *peculium*.

One consequence of the fact that a paterfamilias had power over his slaves and children was that any property and any rights acquired by them immediately vested in him. They served merely as channels by which contractual entitlements flowed to and vested in the paterfamilias. This was a feature of the most crucial importance where the paterfamilias wished to enter into contracts at a distance. By sending a slave or a child there, he could himself acquire contractual rights in dealings entered into many miles from Rome. The importance of this can hardly be exaggerated. For a business of any great scale, it is improbable that a paterfamilias would have, or would have adopted, sufficient children to run it. Accordingly, slaves would play the major part.

In passing, it is important to clarify the scope of one piece of legislation which might otherwise be thought to have restricted the role which sons could play in commerce. The *senatus consultum Macedonianum*, passed under the emperor Vespasian, prohibited loans to sons in paternal power, regardless of their age. According to Ulpian, the reason was that one borrower, Macedo, had found it necessary, in order to repay his creditors, to come into his money sooner rather than later and had therefore murdered his paterfamilias (*D.* 14.6.1 pr.). To discourage others from following this course, the *senatus consultum* prohibited lenders – even after the death of the paterfamilias – from recovering money lent to sons. A permanent defence against any claim for repayment was given, and this was expressly conceived as being for the purpose of penalizing the moneylender (Marcian, *D.* 12.6.40 pr.; Ulpian, *D.* 14.6.9.4). The market in such loans must therefore immediately have disappeared. Interpreted literally, this legislation would have brought all dealings with sons to a halt. But it was accepted that it did not apply where the paterfamilias had appointed his son to carry on trade or authorized him to do so from his *peculium* (both of these possibilities are discussed in the next section). It also applied only to loans and not to other transactions unless they were loans in disguise; and only if the creditor knew or ought to have known that he was lending to a son in power (Ulpian, *D.* 14.6.3 pr. and 3; Pomponius, *D.* 14.6.19).

2. Liability and limitation

The peculium

The praetor's innovation consisted in allowing creditors of slaves or dependent children to bring an *actio de peculio* against their paterfamilias. This was an ordinary action based on the contractual obligation entered into by the slave or child, but it had the special feature that it was limited to the maximum of the amount in the *peculium*. Accordingly, the creditor could have recourse against the paterfamilias not to the full extent of the debtor's obligation but only up to a maximum of the amount in the *peculium*. The result was that, when faced with creditors' claims, the paterfamilias was not subject to bankruptcy proceedings in the normal manner but was at risk only to the extent of the property which he had permitted the slave or dependent child to hold *in peculio*.

This action was available only for acts done by a person under the power of a paterfamilias and was based mainly, but not purely, on relations of status. It did not depend on any authority or task being delegated by the paterfamilias to the child or slave; nor did it depend on the paterfamilias knowing that the business was being carried on. Instead, it depended on the revocable grant of a fund of property to a person who stood in a certain relationship of status to the paterfamilias: commerce and status were therefore intertwined.

There are two important qualifications.

(1) Actions based on the *peculium* were relevant only to the dealings of the child or slave with property or under contracts. Where a dependent member of the paterfamilias's family committed a civil wrong (a delict), such as theft, assault, or damage to property, the paterfamilias was automatically liable to pay the damages, although he could limit his liability by surrendering the wrongdoing child or slave to the person who had been wronged ('noxal surrender'). But the *peculium* had nothing to do with cases of this sort.

(2) The *actio de peculio* was appropriate only where the paterfamilias did not know of the business being carried on. By contrast, where he did know of the business, the praetor gave creditors the benefit of another procedure, the *actio tributoria*, which was slightly less advantageous to the paterfamilias. In each case, however, the main point is the same: in the action the value of the property in the *peculium* or within the particular business acted as a ceiling on the paterfamilias's liability.

Actio institoria *and* actio exercitoria

The praetor introduced two further actions which were important in business dealings: they allowed creditors to sue the owner or principal of a business rather than the 'agent' with whom they had actually dealt. (The terms 'principal' and 'agent' are used loosely.) The first, the 'action on shipping' (*actio exercitoria*), was specific to shipping and allowed a claim against a ship owner (*exercitor*) for the acts of the ship's captain. The second, the 'action on agency' (*actio institoria*), was generally available and allowed a claim against a person who had placed an 'agent' or *institor* in charge of a business, for acts done by the agent in the course of the business. Two general points are worth noting. First, since these actions allowed customers to sue the owner of the business, whom they might never have seen before, they involved a breach of the fundamental principle that an obligation was strictly personal and bound only the person who had undertaken it. Second, the actual agent, the *institor* or captain, might be of any status: free, or in the power of a paterfamilias, or a slave. In each case the owner of the business had unlimited liability for the acts done by the agent in the course of the business. Where the agent was a slave – who could not be personally liable in contract – these actions were the customer's only remedy. On the other hand, if the agent was a free person, he or she would be personally bound by the contract and could be sued upon it, so these actions simply offered an additional remedy, an alternative defendant from whom the creditor could attempt to recover. Since the employer would on the whole be better able to satisfy a claim than the employee, this must none the less have been the customer's remedy of first resort (*D.* 14.1 and 3; Pugliese 1957; di Porto 1984; Aubert 1994).

The circumstances in which liability under these two actions could arise were restricted by the terms of appointment (or *praepositio*) of the *institor* or captain: to use modern (though Latin-derived) terms, by the authority given by the principal to the agent. It was therefore open to the principal, by suitably restrictive drafting of the terms of appointment, to limit the circumstances in which liability came home to him at all.

Ulpian, in his discussion of the *actio institoria*, states that 'not every transaction with an *institor* binds the person who appointed him, but it does so only if the contract was made on account of the business of which he was put in charge' (*D.* 14.3.5.11). There are other statements to the same effect. The principal could also reduce the scope of, or avoid, a liability that would otherwise arise, by giving express notice to parties contracting with his agent; there is a certain amount of discussion about what language such notices must be in, and how large and visible they must be. But it is a matter of contracting out of a liability which would otherwise exist. Plainly, the effectiveness of this limit on the principal's liability turns on how strictly the terms of the appointment are interpreted. The Roman approach was a rather narrow one (*D.* 14.1.7; *D.* 14.3.13 pr.). Accordingly, a certain degree of protection was afforded by suitably tight drafting of the terms of the agent's or captain's appointment. But if, for example, the agent or captain ran up huge losses within the terms of his appointment, the principal was without any protection. Where there was a significant degree of risk, it still made sense to rely on slaves or dependent children rather than independent labour: only that could offer a set financial limit on liability.

Ignorance – a good thing

If a slave or dependent child was running a business, whether the owner or paterfamilias was liable without limit under one of these actions or only up to the amount of the *peculium* depended on the paterfamilias's relationship with the business. The Digest texts make it plain that the paterfamilias was liable up to the amount in the *peculium* even if he had no idea what his slave or child was doing. On the other hand, a principal was liable to the *actio exercitoria* or *institoria* only if he had actually placed the agent in charge of the business, or the captain in charge of the ship, and thereby shown his intention that it should be operated. In short, the paterfamilias could enjoy a financial limit on liability only where he did not appoint the slave or child to do anything, but remained at arm's length from the business. So the apparent advantage of limited liability offered by slaves and dependent children is only that: apparent. In fact, in order to gain that advantage the paterfamilias had to stay at arm's length from the business and not appoint anyone to do anything. The law therefore encouraged a *laissez-faire* attitude on the part of the paterfamilias.

It may be that the explanation of this apparent conundrum lies in the *servus vicarius*. The *peculium* of a slave (a *servus ordinarius*) often included other slaves (known as *servi vicarii*); their *peculia* might equally contain slaves; and so *ad infinitum*. It is here that limitation of liability is able to play its true and effective role. The facts of one text from the Digest will serve as an example. Ulpian deals with the case where the shipowner (to use the term loosely) is not an independent person but is in the power of another person: he is a slave or dependent child. He therefore does not own the ship but simply has it in his *peculium*. He appoints a captain to run the ship. This involves one more layer than the basic case: not just shipowner and captain, but shipowner's paterfamilias, shipowner and captain. The main consequence is that anybody wishing to bring the *actio exercitoria* based on what the captain does will have to bring it not against the shipowner but against his paterfamilias. Ulpian draws a distinction: if the shipowner is carrying on that business by the will (*voluntas*) of his paterfamilias, then the action can be brought against the paterfamilias without limitation. On the other hand, if the business is not being carried on by the will of the paterfamilias but by the will of the dependent shipowner, the paterfamilias is liable only up to the value in the shipowner's *peculium* (*D.* 14.1.1.19).

Here we see the true significance of the rules described earlier. There is unlimited liability for acts done by the captain or manager within his terms of appointment, but this is true only at the level of the person who appointed him. The liability to which the ultimate owner of the ship or business is exposed is limited by the value of the *peculium* of the slave or dependant responsible for appointing the captain or business manager. That might be a dependant several degrees removed from the ultimate owner himself.

The legal sources therefore suggest that, depending on the level of risk involved in any particular enterprise, it would – ideally – be appropriate to have the enterprise managed not just by slaves or other dependent labour but by slaves who stood at some remove from the paterfamilias

by reason of belonging to the *peculium* of one of his
offered the advantage that the paterfamilias had no
them to do anything, and might indeed have no knc
what they were doing. When we consider how busi
at least by the wealthy, we should therefore be awar
which *servi vicarii* had to offer. The law presents signi
businesses organized in the shape of a pyramid, wi
at the apex and below him layers of managers and
archy also makes realistic the possibility that the owner of the slaves
might have little idea what each was doing; and that itself justifies the
central role played in the jurists' discussions by considerations about
intention and will in determining the extent of the paterfamilias's
liability.

Of course, the fact that this approach maximizes the advantages of
one trader means that it also minimizes those of his trading partners. It
follows that whether in fact a trader will be able to deal with his trading
partners on such advantageous terms – or whether, for example, they
will insist on his undertaking personal or unlimited liability in a transaction – will turn on their respective bargaining strengths. Accordingly, in
reality the points mentioned so far would not be the only factors at work.

3. Independent labour

Slave labour was not the only labour available at Rome (Garnsey 1980).
Independent employees acted as individuals and acquired rights solely
for themselves. If they entered into a contract with somebody, there was
no question of those contractual rights automatically vesting in their
employer. This is quite different from the conception of agency with
which we are now familiar, for example, in Scots and English law, where
the acts of the agent can actually create contractual relations between
the employer and the third party with whom the agent deals. In these
systems the employer or 'principal' does not have, for example, to have
the agent assign his contractual rights to him. But in Roman law the
employer did not enjoy this advantage. It is true that there would be no
great difficulty in setting up another contract by which the independent
employee agreed to transfer to his employer any rights he might acquire.
Yet this would introduce an additional step into the situation which
might cause problems: the only person who would be entitled to sue the
third party would be the employee, who contracted with him; and if the
employee became insolvent, it would be of little use to the employer to

right of action against him. All these anxieties could be removed, however, by the simple expedient of making use of dependent labour: children and slaves. Probably until the early third century, there were advantages in using dependent labour for purposes of agency. Put simply, since the dependent agent was as a matter of law identified with the paterfamilias himself, to use such labour was in effect to cut out the middle-man.

None the less, the legal sources alone provide plenty of evidence of the employment of independent people, especially freedmen, sometimes doing the same jobs as they had done when they were previously slaves. Equally, there are faint signs of developments in the law making it easier to employ free people. From the second century AD, there was a slow but sure recognition that it was possible for one person to acquire rights through a free person, a procurator. This is said to have been more or less accepted in the case of acquiring possession at about the end of the first century AD (Neratius, *D.* 41.3.41). Certainly by the third century any doubts seem to have been overcome.

More generally, in the writings of the jurist Papinian at the end of the second century or beginning of the third, there are clear indications that actions might be available, on account of dealings carried out by a procurator, both for and against his employer. This does not mean that independent agents had not been used before. But it is probably right to detect in this development that a need had been perceived and was being gradually addressed by the law, to make remedies available between the parties genuinely interested in a transaction, and not to make the efficacy of remedies dependent on contingencies such as the solvency of the procurator. It may also be right to see in this development signs of what is sometimes called the 'juridification' of relationships: the incorporation within a legal framework of relations which had previously been based purely on *amicitia* or *officium*. However that may be, what is clear is that in a system which had wholeheartedly favoured the employment of dependent labour, the balance was being redressed to make the employment of independent labour more straightforward.

4. Partnership

One of the consensual contracts developed by Roman law was that of partnership (*societas*). It is quite clear that the background to this was far from commercial: the earliest precursor of partnership was an arrangement under which co-heirs of an inheritance continued to own and administer it in common. This seems to have left its mark on the law of *societas*, as it eventually developed, since one form of partnership was a partnership 'of all property' (*omnium bonorum*) which seems most unsuitable for commercial purposes.

None the less, it was possible to enter into a partnership for one line of business only or for a single transaction, and this would bring the advantages of combining the skills and expertise, and not least the capital, of the partners. Apart from ordinary commercial ventures, a typical instance of partnership in the late republic was that of tax collectors (*publicani*); to some extent this was governed by special rules (Buckland 1963: 513).

The partners were free to make whatever terms they would for sharing profits and losses, except that it was not permitted to have a partner who shared only in the losses and not in the profits. In the absence of other provision, shares in profits and losses were equal. A Dacian document of AD 167 sets out terms for a partnership in – so far as its fragmentary state reveals – some detail. Oddly enough, it then goes on to confirm them by means of a *stipulatio*. Since the document contains only a *stipulatio* by one of the partners undertaking obligations to the other, it seems most likely that another, reciprocal version of the document would also have been produced. The alternative is that the document simply betrays a misunderstanding of the law (*FIRA* 3.157).

To modern eyes the most striking feature of the Roman partnership is that the only people on whom it normally had any effect were the partners. To the outside world its existence was of no significance: so if one partner entered into a contract to sell goods, he alone was bound by the contract. The partnership agreement mattered only to him and his partner, since under it he might be obliged to communicate to his partner some of the benefits he derived from the contract. The only exception to this rule would be if the other party to the contract (in this example the buyer) could show that the partner with whom he had dealt had been acting as the agent (*institor*) of the other: in that case, as explained already, he could sue the 'principal' partner, even though he had had no dealings directly with him. For these reasons, although the possibility of entering into a partnership brought advantages in terms of sharing costs and resources, it brought no particular benefit as a means of structuring a business.

5. Some conclusions on business organization

The development of the law of agency through procurators certainly made it easier to make use of independent labour within the organization of a business. Equally, the adoption of a strict approach to interpreting the terms on which an *institor* or captain had been appointed made it possible with appropriate drafting to make use of them for specific highly specialized purposes, without giving too much of a hostage to fortune. But there was still no substitute for making use of a slave or dependant at critical junctures of the business, particularly in high-risk activities, because only they could offer the advantage of a limitation to the value of their *peculium*.

The legal advantages of a *laissez-faire* approach to business fit rather well with what is known about social attitudes to trade. There is plenty of evidence in the Digest and elsewhere of a healthy disdain for involvement in trade. There were also restrictions on the extent to which senators could engage in trade (Talbert 1984: 45–6). These are of course issues quite different from benefiting, or drawing the profits, from trade: the aristocracy may not itself have traded, but it certainly took the profits from trade (Plutarch, *Cato maior* 21.6–7; Whittaker 1993: 58). That picture – of keeping a safe distance from trade – is complemented by the conclusions drawn here from the legal sources: not simply (as is well known) that it was possible to trade by means of intermediaries, but also that there were positive advantages to be had by reducing one's level of involvement and knowledge of the business and to confining oneself to enjoying profits vicariously. We can draw some comfort from the fact that social attitudes and legal rules point towards the same kind of organization of business, along *laissez-faire* lines. This suggests that the law is not operating here in its own remote world of isolated rules but is firmly anchored in the realities of Roman life and the demands at least of its well-heeled citizens.

VI INSOLVENCY

The law of insolvency has a significant bearing on commercial enterprise, since, when contemplating taking risks, all but the boldest will reflect for a moment on the consequences of financial disaster. In Rome they were rather serious. There were two ways in which a creditor could enforce a debt owed to him: execution against the person of the debtor and execution against his property. The details of personal execution are uncertain. It seems unlikely that a deeply obscure provision of the Twelve Tables (3.6) – 'let them cut up their shares' (*partes secanto*) actually referred, as used to be believed (perhaps by those who had recently read *The Merchant of Venice*), to the creditors carving up the debtor's body rather than his assets. But what personal execution did mean was that the debtor, although not enslaved, was in the power of the creditor and could be imprisoned. It may be that this continued until he had worked off his debt, although this is not certain.

In classical times, the normal procedure seems to have been execution against the debtor's property. Even this was extremely drastic. A creditor who was not satisfied could seek an order from the praetor for seizure of the debtor's whole property. Fortified with this order, the creditor could then take possession and administer the property on behalf of all the creditors of the debtor; the granting of the order was publicized, presumably to allow other creditors to join the proceedings. This stage was typically followed by a public auction of the debtor's whole property, in which the property was knocked down to the bidder who offered the creditors the highest dividend on their claims. The procedure was called *bonorum venditio* (Gaius, *Inst.* 3.78–9).

From the creditors' point of view, it seems clear that this sort of system could hardly have been guaranteed to produce the best return: it might well have been possible to sell specific items of property for more, individually. But the notion that seems to lie beneath this system is that, with the exception of privileged creditors such as the fisc or certain municipalities (Plin., *ep.* 10.108–9), all creditors must be treated in the same way. For that reason the praetor introduced a series of remedies which made it possible to undo a transaction under which one creditor had knowingly benefited at the expense of the others within the year preceding insolvency (Kaser 1971: 251–2).

From the debtor's point of view, the remarkable – and very harsh – feature of this system was that the sale was not only of items of the debtor's property sufficient to meet the debt (as would, for example, typically be the case nowadays), and it made no difference that one or two items in his estate might satisfy it: the whole had to be sold up. Behind this system is a notion of bankruptcy quite different from our own: the modern conception in Britain is that the debtor's estate should be taken out of his control and administered by a trustee, in order to realize the assets and satisfy the creditors as far as possible. In contrast, in the Roman approach lurks the idea that the debtor must be punished. Two further points support this view. First, the fact that the proceedings made the debtor *infamis*, not quite the same as 'infamous', but a state which (crucially) involved social stigma, as well as some civil disabilities, such as being unable to be a judge, to appoint an agent to conduct litigation, or as a rule to conduct litigation on behalf of anyone other than oneself (Kaser 1996: 194, 208, 212, 383–403).

Second, Augustus (or possibly Caesar) introduced a procedure, *bonorum cessio*, which mitigated the harshness of this regime to some extent. The significance of the introduction of this measure at a time when there was serious indebtedness at the highest levels in society cannot be doubted (de Neeve 1984: 154–7). The details of the procedure are not well known, but its availability may have been restricted to those who were not at fault for their insolvency. Under this procedure the debtor voluntarily surrendered his property to the creditors; the consequence was that he did not become *infamis* and was also not liable to execution against his person; but the whole of his property was still affected (*D.* 42.3; Kaser 1996: 405–7; Pakter 1994).

A procedure under which only items of property sufficient to meet the debt were sold up became routinely available under the *cognitio* system of procedure, which gained ground throughout the principate but appears to have superseded the formulary procedure only in the third century. Prior to that, however, though at an uncertain date, a *senatus consultum* had apparently permitted *clarae personae*, members of the senatorial class, to enjoy such a privilege. They therefore could avoid the worst rigours of insolvency; and under this procedure they did not become *infames* either. But that was not the normal rule for the classical system of procedure (Kaser 1996: 404–5).

With failure bringing this unattractive prospect into view, it seems likely that a Roman would have taken great care to structure business dealings so as to avoid the risk of personal insolvency and the sale of his entire personal property. Whether these rules inhibited commerce as a whole is a question which it is really impossible to answer.

VII CONCLUSIONS

The orthodoxy is that the Roman economy was undeveloped; and evidence for the extent and importance of trade and commerce is inadequate (Garnsey and Saller 1987: 43, 47). It is true that in Roman times trade and business were relatively insignificant compared with land. But they were not neglected by the law. Although it is conceivable that the jurists might have created a mass of commercial law in the absence of any significant commercial practice in which to employ it, it does seem doubtful whether they would have developed structures and rules of much sophistication if their economy went little beyond exchange for purposes of subsistence.

Yet the sorts of structures and rules considered in this chapter are of considerable sophistication. Although some relics of the past remained, such as the impossibility of sales of generic goods and some inconveniences in the law of real security, mostly these can be understood and could be overcome: for example, because *stipulatio* would be used for a generic sale and personal security would regularly be used in preference to real security.

The documents of practice also indicate that complex commercial transactions did not take place purely in the imagination of the jurists. Many of the documents demonstrate remarkable fidelity to the law described in the legal sources. It is, however, also true that the documents throw up puzzles which the legal sources do not. To conclude with just one: it is common to think of 'good faith' contracts as having the advantage of simplicity. But what practice seems to confirm beyond question is the continuing vitality and importance of the formal contract of *stipulatio*. Time and again what we find in practice is a detailed contract (such as the sales, building contracts and partnerships mentioned above) confirmed by a *stipulatio*. This means that the parties gave up the apparent benefits of the good faith contract – ease of formation, implied terms, a less rigid procedural regime (see the next chapter) – in favour of a contract which required to be entered into formally, the parties (or their representatives) face to face, and which would be interpreted strictly. The message is not unambiguous. It is not possible to decipher it with any conviction here. But it does at least seem possible that to the Romans the archetype of contract remained the formal promise, and the strictness with which it was interpreted offered the welcome benefit of certainty.

CHAPTER 6

Litigation

The last three chapters have been concerned with substantive law: the rules which governed everyday life and its transactions. But, in the end, the question whether a person enjoys a particular right comes down to whether he or she is able to enforce it in practice. This is where the issue of procedure, of litigation, is important. The first section of this chapter gives a sketch of the workings of the various Roman civil procedures in the classical period; to a large extent this is confined to the bare facts. The second section then attempts to draw out the significance of the procedural rules for the vindication of rights in practice, and also deals briefly with access to the courts and legal representation.

I CIVIL PROCEDURE IN THE CLASSICAL PERIOD

1. Formulary procedure

The standard classical civil procedure is known as the formulary system, for reasons which will become obvious. It was neither the first nor the last of the Roman civil procedural systems, but it held sway for most of the classical period; the writings of the leading jurists were written in connexion with it; and to some degree they depend on understanding it.

Characteristic of formulary procedure is that it took place in two stages, the first before the praetor, the magistrate charged with the administration of justice, and the second before a judge. To initiate civil litigation a plaintiff had to obtain a formula from the praetor, which encapsulated the essence of the dispute. This could be done only in the presence of the intended defendant, since the defendant too had to have some say in what was included in the formula. The case was then sent by the praetor for trial before a judge. The formula set out the full extent of the issue or issues to be decided by the judge on the evidence. The judge was given authority by the praetor to judge only on the issue as set

out in the formula; and nothing else was either relevant or w
judge's competence to determine. This two-stage procedure be
resemblance to Athenian procedure, in which the appropriat
trate, the *archon*, conducted an inquiry into the facts (*anakrisis*) an
at an issue which was to be put before the court; in the second stage of
proceedings the parties appeared and made their speeches before the
court (Sealey 1994: 118–19; Todd 1993: 126–7). The difference was that
the Athenian court consisted of many judges, not just one.

Getting the defendant before the praetor

Since the procedure could not commence without the defendant, it was
necessary to have a means of compelling his attendance before the
praetor, a stage of proceedings known as proceedings *in iure*. The
opening provisions of the Twelve Tables were already concerned with
this (they are cited in chapter 1).

Under the formulary system, it was not uncommon for the parties to
agree to meet at a certain place for the purpose of then going before
the praetor to obtain a formula. The prospective defendant would
promise to appear at a certain place and time near the court, so that
the plaintiff could then formally summon him before the magistrate (*in
ius vocatio*). A number of surviving documents deal precisely with this
(Wolf 1985).

There was nothing necessarily extended about these proceedings: on
the whole the praetor did not investigate the rights or wrongs of the
matter but simply granted a formula which covered the pleas of each
party. There was, however, a group of cases in which the formula would
be granted only after scrutiny of the case; and if the plaintiff sought an
action which did not appear in the edict this too would presumably
require more time.

The formula

In book 4 of his Institutes Gaius gives a clear account of the way in
which formulae were composed (*Inst.* 4.39–52; see also Jolowicz and
Nicholas 1972: 203–15). The essence is this: formulae were built up of
clauses, some mandatory, others optional, so as to encapsulate in a single
sentence all the issues which the judge must determine. The judge was
therefore faced with an (admittedly complex) question to which the
answer must in effect be 'yes' or 'no'. Plainly this limited his scope for
error; not an unimportant consideration, given that he would be a lay
judge. Some examples should help.

A basic formula

Here is the formula for the basic action for recovery of property, the *vindicatio*, discussed in chapter 4:

> Let Gaius be judge. If it appears that the slave which is at issue belongs to Aulus Agerius at civil law, and it has not in the opinion of the judge been restored to Aulus Agerius, whatever its value shall be let the judge condemn Numerius Negidius to pay that to Aulus Agerius; if it does not so appear, let him absolve.

The formula necessarily begins with the appointment of the judge, in this case Gaius. It is this sentence which gives him authority, which as a private citizen rather than an official he would not otherwise have, to determine the dispute. The stock names used for the parties to the action are conventional, playing on words: the plaintiff because he sues (*agere*), the defendant because he denies or refuses to pay or both (*negare, numerare*). This formula faces the judge with the task of assessing whether the slave does belong to the plaintiff at civil law or not. We shall return to the judge's decision shortly.

A modified formula

It has already been mentioned that the defendant must be present when the formula was issued; the reason is that the parties must agree what all the issues between them were, and it might be appropriate for defences put forward by the defendant to be inserted as additional clauses in the formula. Take the example of the basic action for payment of a sum owed (*condictio*), which would be used in the case of a loan (*mutuum*) or *stipulatio* of a sum of money:

> Let Gaius be judge. If it appears that Numerius Negidius ought to give Aulus Agerius 1,000 sesterces, let the judge condemn Numerius Negidius to Aulus Agerius for 1,000 sesterces; if it does not so appear, let him absolve.

This is an entirely straightforward formula. But what should be noted is that the formula as it stands will allow the defendant to advance only one defence: that he does not owe the money. Suppose, however, that he admits he owes the money but alleges that the parties had made an agreement that for a period of five years the plaintiff would not sue for repayment. To raise this issue before the court, so as to be entitled to lead witnesses or produce other evidence about it, the defendant will have to plead a further defence. Here the appropriate one would be the defence that there was an agreement (*exceptio pacti*): the words 'unless it was agreed between Aulus Agerius and Numerius Negidius that no action for this money should be brought for five years' would simply be added to the formula.

Similarly, if the defendant admitted the debt but alleged that he was tricked by the plaintiff into entering into the contract, he would have to plead a defence. Here the appropriate one might be the *exceptio doli*, which was a general plea to the effect that the plaintiff was acting fraudulently or in bad faith: the words 'if in this matter nothing has been or is being done in bad faith by Aulus Agerius' would be added to the formula.

The pleading of a defence (*exceptio*) by the defendant may well not have been the end of the matter: the plaintiff might have wished to plead a further point in reply to it. This would be known as a 'reply' (*replicatio*); a further reply by the defendant would be a *triplicatio* (more or less untranslatable); and so *ad infinitum*. Here is the formula for the *actio Publiciana*, which was discussed in chapter 4. This version includes the modifications necessary to reflect the fact that the action is being brought by the bonitary owner of a slave against the true owner, and the true owner has pleaded his civil-law title as a defence.

Let Gaius be judge. If Aulus Agerius had for one year possessed the slave which he bought in good faith and which was delivered to him, then if that slave which is at issue would have belonged to him at civil law, unless the slave which is at issue belongs at civil law to Numerius Negidius, and Numerius Negidius did not sell and deliver the slave at issue to Aulus Agerius, and it has not in the opinion of the judge been restored to Aulus Agerius, whatever its value shall be let the judge condemn Numerius Negidius to pay that to Aulus Agerius; if it does not so appear, let him absolve.

The resemblance between this formula and the basic *vindicatio* with which we began is clear. One can therefore get an impression of the versatility of this system of pleading, where a new block is added to the formula to deal with a new complexity, and there is in effect no limit to the ultimate extent of the formula. It has of course to be conceded that the longer and more complex the formula became, the more problematic it must have been for a lay judge to apply it. Help would be required.

Discretion

Some actions were known as 'good faith actions' (*bonae fidei iudicia*). This was true of all of the most important contracts, with the exception of *stipulatio* and the loan of *mutuum* (for both of which, provided the *stipulatio* was for a fixed sum of money, the appropriate action was the *condictio* mentioned above). The formulae for good faith actions – unlike the *condictio* – included specific reference to good faith. Here is the formula for the buyer's action under the contract of sale.

Let Gaius be judge. Whereas Aulus Agerius bought from Numerius Negidius the slave which is at issue, whatever as a matter of good faith Numerius Negidius ought to give to or do for Aulus Agerius, let the judge condemn Numerius Negidius to Aulus Agerius in respect of that; if it does not so appear, let him absolve.

The significance of this reference to good faith was that the judge had much more discretion: he was not left simply to determine whether 1,000 sesterces were owed or not owed but was able to decide exactly what the defendant ought to pay. The most important consequence of the reference to good faith was that there was no need for a defendant to plead defences – such as that there had been an agreement or that the plaintiff was acting fraudulently – since the judge would be able to take evidence about these into account anyway, simply as a matter of applying the standard of good faith.

Non-standard formulae

The praetor's edict contained only the standard formulae. Not all cases would be covered. It was possible none the less for a plaintiff to seek a formula even in a novel case. In these instances the formula would often set out the facts on which the plaintiff relied, rather than the brief legal narrative given in the examples already mentioned. Actions with formulae of this sort were known as *actiones in factum* or *actiones utiles*, and were particularly important in extending the law. For example, the Digest title on the *lex Aquilia* (*D.* 9.2) frequently refers to such actions: this was because they were of the greatest significance in bringing up to date and expanding the scope of a statute which had been drafted in rather narrow terms. The statute itself gave a remedy in damages only to the owner of a thing which had been harmed, and only where loss had been directly caused; *actiones in factum* or *actiones utiles* extended the scope of liability in this area and so, for instance, gave a remedy to other people who had interests in the thing, and for loss which had been indirectly caused.

From praetor to judge

Once the formula was settled and the judge appointed, the praetor's role was over, and the parties' dispute went before a judge or *iudex* (proceedings *apud iudicem*). The task for the judge was to hear the evidence led by the parties in order to determine whether he should condemn the defendant to pay or absolve him.

Judgment in money

The judgment would simply be a determination whether the plaintiff had proved the necessary facts set out in the formula: in effect, this was a 'yes or no' decision by the judge, since he need only pronounce that the defendant was condemned or that he was absolved. In actions where the formula was not directed at a fixed sum, the judge would also need to make an assessment of the amount the defendant must pay the plaintiff.

No reasons were given in the judgment, nor was any appeal possible against it (although it might in exceptional circumstances be set aside as void). It would be difficult in any case to appeal against a judgment without knowing how the judge had arrived at it.

It was fundamental to the formulary system that the only judgments the judge could pronounce were monetary. It did not matter that what the plaintiff really wanted was the return of his property; the judge was able only to award a sum of money.

There was a device, however, for encouraging the defendant to return the property rather than paying its value. It is reflected in the formula of certain actions by the presence of what is known as the *clausula arbitraria* ('discretionary clause'). The clause simply provided 'and it has not in the opinion of the judge been restored to the plaintiff'; this appears, for instance, in the formula for the *vindicatio* quoted earlier. The presence of this clause allowed the judge, when he had concluded that the plaintiff was the owner, to delay pronouncing judgment against the defendant if he returned the object. If he did, no judgment was pronounced. If he did not, the judge would ask the plaintiff to value the object. Although the plaintiff had to swear an oath as to the value of the object, it seems clear that he or she could err on the side of generosity; after all this was expropriation of the plaintiff's property. The upshot was that, if the defendant elected not to return the object, he would have to pay an inflated value for it. Indirectly, therefore, some pressure was put on him to perform rather than pay.

This clause appeared in other actions besides the *vindicatio*: for example, in the action for warding off rainwater discussed in chapter 4. Its presence there again gave a defendant whom the judge had provisionally found liable an incentive to take down the construction that was causing rainwater to damage the plaintiff's land. If he did so, judgment would not be pronounced against him.

This seems a very cumbersome method, which prompts the question: why? The answer probably lies in the fact that the judge was a lay judge:

once he had pronounced his judgment, he had no further power. He had
no chance to supervise what then happened, and no standing to do so.
He had no court officials to execute the judgment or to provide means
for its enforcement. A monetary judgment was a straightforward end of
the proceedings so far as he was concerned; if its enforcement involved
the insolvency of the defendant, that was a matter for the praetor.

The question arises whether the monetary judgment was of greater
advantage to the plaintiff or the defendant. Both views have been held;
and a good deal must turn on the ease with which the defendant could
come up with money, and so to some extent on how scarce money was
(Kelly 1966: 73–84; de Neeve 1984: 154–7). It is clear enough from literary sources that from time to time there were monetary crises (for
instance, in 88 BC, 66–63 BC, 49–45 BC and AD 33; Duncan-Jones 1994:
20–32), and no doubt in those periods a defendant might find it particularly convenient to return the property rather than pay. Apart from this,
it seems doubtful whether there is much to be gained by generalization:
everything must have turned on the particular parties and property
involved.

Execution of judgments

The execution of a judgment was either personal (against the person of
the judgment debtor) or real (against his property). The system was
described in section VI of chapter 5 in the context of insolvency.

2. Other procedures

The praetor was not confined to granting formulae for actions going to
trial but was also as part of his power of jurisdiction empowered to grant
orders of other types. It is worth noting the most important ones here;
they have been mentioned where appropriate in earlier chapters.

(1) Interdicts. The praetor's edict contained a lengthy list of interdicts;
book 43 of the Digest contains titles on thirty-three of them. They range
widely. Interdicts were of exceptional importance in the law of property,
where they regulated not just possession (*D.* 43.16, 17 and 31) but also
rights of way, water and watercourses, drains, overhanging branches,
windfall fruit from trees and other such things (*D.* 43.18, 20–3, 27–8).
Some of them have already been discussed in chapter 4. Other interdicts
were concerned largely with questions of municipal administration: preventing building in public or sacred places; enabling road repairs to be
carried out; preserving access to public waterways (*D.* 43.6–15).

The principal advantage of interdict proceedings was that they were swift. This was to a large degree because they were primarily concerned with preserving the status quo and involved no inquiry into the merits of the case. So, for example, someone could obtain an interdict to prevent his neighbour building, or interfering with his water supply, or carrying out any activity contrary to his prohibition: in each case the praetor was prepared to maintain the status quo by granting the interdict. The person seeking the interdict need not show entitlement, but simply a *prima facie* case, for example that he had been accustomed to use the water source.

(2) 'Sending into possession' (*missio in possessionem*) was a remedy made available by the praetor in a wide range of circumstances: examples include the safeguarding of a legacy where there was doubt about the heir's solvency; where a neighbour sought possession to secure himself against the threatened collapse of an adjacent building (*damnum infectum*: see chapter 4); and also as a preliminary step to insolvency proceedings (see chapter 5).

(3) *Restitutio in integrum*. This remedy, which means roughly 'restoration of the status quo', was a means by which the praetor could relieve someone of the consequences of a transaction into which he or she had entered. The best-known example was mentioned in chapter 3, namely the relief of minors who had been imposed upon or deceived into entering a transaction. But the praetor also offered this remedy in general to people who had entered into a transaction under the influence of fraud or duress. The effect was in each case that the transaction was set aside.

3. Other civil jurisdictions

Although the Digest gives the strong impression that litigation was a matter of appearing before a single judge, a few words should be said here about two other civil jurisdictions which operated in the classical period (for further discussion, see Kelly 1976).

(1) *Recuperatores* ('recoverers'). A court of *recuperatores* was essentially a court composed of several persons eligible to be appointed as judges, usually but not always three. The cases in which recuperatorial procedure was appropriate are not quite clear, although they were supposed to involve a greater public interest than ordinary cases. The *lex Irnitana* indicates that there was a known list of cases or categories of case which went before *recuperatores*: it says that at Irni cases which would in Rome

be heard by *recuperatores* should be treated in the same way at Irni (*lex Irn.* ch. 89). But we are not told which cases were on this list.

(2) *Centumviri*. Details about the court of *centumviri* (literally, 100 men) lack. It seems to have sat in divisions rather than as a whole, but the numbers sitting were clearly large. Its jurisdiction was very limited. Two of its principal concerns were evidently cases where inheritances in excess of a certain value were being claimed and cases where the validity of wills was being challenged, again probably only where the estate exceeded a certain value. The ancient sources indicate that the centumviral court was the forum for forensic advocacy, and that there might be considerable public interest in litigation there (Cic., *de oratore* 1.180; Plin., *ep.* 6.33.3; Quintilian, *inst.* 12.5.6; Crook 1995: 181, 184–5).

4. Provincial practice

In the provinces, it was the provincial governor who exercised jurisdiction. As already mentioned in chapter 1, there are marked similarities between his role and that of the praetor at Rome; and jurisdiction was exercised in accordance with the governor's edict.

It does not appear, however, that in the provinces the two-stage formulary procedure was normally used. Instead, provincial jurisdiction seems to have operated under a single-stage procedure in which the governor or a deputy appointed by him heard the whole of each case. It seems probable that this is one of the roots of the various systems of nonformulary civil procedure which became established in the later classical period (see below). The provincial governor evidently went on circuit around the province; the *lex Irnitana* provides for promises for appearance to be made before him at the place where he is expected to be on the day in question (*lex Irn.* ch. 84).

5. Municipal jurisdictions

Municipal magistrates (or *duoviri*) also had a limited jurisdiction, under the supervision of the praetor (in Italy) or appropriate provincial governor. The details of this have become fairly clear since the discovery of the *lex Irnitana*. It contains provisions on the limits which applied to the jurisdiction of the local magistrates, and provisions for appointing judges and *recuperatores* and arranging for trials to begin. Actions which exceeded the jurisdiction of the local magistrates had to be remitted to the provincial governor. In Irni this applied in particular to actions which concerned or raised an issue about a person's freedom, and to so-called 'infaming' actions, that is, actions condemnation in which involved dishonour (*infamia*) and certain civil disabilities. It is clear that the defendant could agree to an infaming action's being heard locally, although he was not obliged to do so; it is equally clear that under no circumstances could an action involving a person's freedom be heard locally. There was also a financial limit on the jurisdiction of local magistrates: at Irni this was 1,000 sesterces; in larger communities this figure will have been larger. Whether an action for a larger sum could take place there with the agreement of the defendant is disputed (*lex Irn.* 84).

6. Extraordinary proceedings

Ordinary formulary procedure came to be described as the *ordo*; any procedure which fell outside it was *extra ordinem*. The term used for a later type of civil procedure, *cognitio extra ordinem* ('extraordinary *cognitio*'), does not therefore refer to a single unitary procedure but is simply a collective term for completely different procedures whose only common feature was that they did not fall under the ordinary procedure. Provincial governors, for instance, had long exercised their jurisdiction in a way which did not fall within the ordinary procedure: as mentioned already, this is thought to be one of the roots of the *cognitio* procedure.

One instance of a new use of *cognitio* under the principate was the jurisdiction for *fideicommissa*, 'trusts', established by the emperor Augustus (see chapter 3). Rather than leaving them to the ordinary jurisdiction of the praetor, he entrusted *fideicommissa* to the consuls, magistrates who ordinarily played no part in civil jurisdiction. Under Claudius two special *praetores fideicommissarii* were appointed; later this was reduced to one. Their jurisdiction and that of the consuls seem to have been concurrent; probably the consuls dealt only with the most important cases. Regardless which magistrate had jurisdiction, the procedure remained an extraordinary one (Just., *Inst.* 2.23.pr.–1; Pomponius, *D.* 1.2.2.32). Other special praetors for such things as fiscal matters, and various prefects, also exercised jurisdiction which falls within this category. So did the emperor.

The central characteristic of these extraordinary procedures is that they had a single stage only, and the case was not remitted in a separate stage for trial by a judge but was disposed of by the magistrate. In practice a busy magistrate will not have been able to deal with many cases in person, from start to finish, and the practice was therefore to appoint a deputy to determine the case (*iudex pedaneus*). Even the emperor might sit as a judge; again, it is more likely that he would appoint a deputy to sit in his place (Peachin 1996).

The judge was for the first time an official (although still not necessarily a lawyer). But this had an important consequence: for the first time there could be an appeal against the judgment to a higher-ranking official. Ultimate appeal would lie to the emperor as the pinnacle of this hierarchy of officialdom.

Although *cognitio* was conceptually different from the formulary system, the differences between the two systems can be exaggerated. The critical points are that in formulary procedure the parties were entitled to select their own judge, while in *cognitio* they were not; in formulary procedure the magistrate was obliged to appoint someone else as judge, while in *cognitio* he was not; in formulary procedure there was no appeal, while in *cognitio* there was.

It will be clear even from this sketch that *cognitio* had many roots, and that it is not possible to settle on a date at which it became 'the procedure' for civil business. Formulary procedure was formally abandoned only in the fourth century, although it had probably fallen into desuetude by the end of the third (Kaser 1996: 435–45). For much of the classical period the two types of procedure must have co-existed.

II VINDICATION OF RIGHTS IN PRACTICE

The last section attempted to sketch out the workings of the various systems of civil procedure, so far as we are now able to reconstruct them. But an even more difficult task of reconstruction is that of procedure in practice, and how parties would actually have experienced the workings of these systems. Here there are several topics worth considering.

1. Procedural advantage

A knowledge of procedure brings its advantages, first at the stage of setting up arrangements which are intended to produce certain legal effects; and second at the stage of deciding which form of legal action to employ.

Probably the best examples of the first are to be found where two different methods of achieving a result were available, one of which would give rise to an ordinary action under the formulary procedure and the other to an action justiciable under *cognitio extra ordinem*. The clearest

example is probably that of legacies and *fideicommissa.* I
cedure, to which a legatee must resort, only money ju
pronounced, so that the legatee could never be assu
actually obtain the property bequeathed. In the extr
tion responsible for *fideicommissa,* however, the judge c
order for delivery of the actual property. A testator
about these questions, and to whom it was really importa...
beneficiary should receive a specific piece of property rather than its
value, would therefore be inclined – or at least well-advised – to use the
method of *fideicommissum* rather than legacy. Whether this entered into
the calculations of many testators is an open question. This procedural
issue is one which would have arisen only in Roman practice and presumably not in the provinces: there the governor or his deputy disposed
of all cases and will hardly have switched from one procedure to another
according to what sort of case he was hearing.

The second context in which procedural advantage can be exploited
simply involves assessing what must be proved in order to obtain a
remedy and taking the most advantageous course. To take an example
from chapter 4: using the *actio Publiciana* to recover property would be
simpler than using a *vindicatio*; instead of proving absolute ownership,
it would be necessary to prove only that one had acquired possession
in good faith and for a good cause. To use an interdict to recover possession would often (depending on the facts) be simpler still. Similarly,
if a neighbour was constructing a dangerous edifice, the choice would
lie between *operis novi nuntiatio, damnum infectum* and the interdict *quod vi
aut clam*: the first of these would do if the work was still proceeding, the
third if it was not; the second would require that there be some defect
in the construction. The point is simply that knowing your remedy was
a vital part of successful litigation. And the law was sufficiently
complex that knowing your remedy meant knowing a man who did: a
jurist.

2. How easy was it to get the defendant into court?

Suing those who are wealthier and more powerful is never easy, and the
need to do so must have been a deterrent to some would-be litigants. It
may be, however, that this was not the greatest of the plaintiff's
difficulties (though for a different view see Kelly 1966: 6–11, 27–9). The
praetor took measures to preserve the dignity of his own jurisdiction:
where a defendant failed to respond to a summons before him, he was

ated as being in hiding, and the praetor would grant the plaintiff's request for an order giving him possession of the defendant's property (Lenel 1927: 415; Kaser 1996: 222). Once in possession, the plaintiff would be able to take steps to sell property in order to satisfy his claim. Of course, this procedure might be thwarted if the praetor refused to grant the order (an issue to which we shall return), or if the defendant had no property within the jurisdiction. But for many cases it should have been adequate.

The praetor (or, presumably, the provincial governor in the provinces) also stepped in to support the jurisdiction of municipal magistrates, by promulgating an edict for the event that a defendant failed to answer a summons to court. The law was clear: even a defendant who claimed that the court had no jurisdiction over him or the particular case was obliged to answer a summons to it; from there the case would, if appropriate, be remitted to a higher court (Lenel 1927: 51–3).

3. Could magistrates be relied upon?

So far it has been assumed that the praetor could be relied upon, taking legal advice where necessary from jurists, to grant the appropriate formula *sine ira et studio*. But even in the Digest we hear of unfair or incompetent praetors or provincial governors (Paul, *D.* 1.1.11; Papinian, *D.* 29.5.21.2; Maecianus, *D.* 36.1.67.2; Ulpian, *D.* 37.10.3.5). At least so far as incompetence is concerned, matters could be improved by taking advice; and we hear of no less a jurist than Ulpian sitting as assessor to a praetor (Ulpian, *D.* 4.2.9.3). Unfairness must have been a much more intractable problem.

Part of the problem, at least while the edict continued to develop, must have been the immense discretion conferred on the praetor to grant remedies, including remedies which did not appear in the edict itself (actions *in factum*), or to refuse them. In 67 BC a statute, the *lex Cornelia*, was enacted to require praetors to publish their edicts and administer justice in accordance with them. So there was plainly an awareness of the risks of wholly unfettered discretion; yet on the other hand the flexibility of the edict was its chief advantage as a fertile source of new law.

The problem must have been exacerbated by the political nature of the praetor's office: this was just one step in a political career, and advancement to the next step, the consulship, depended at least on retaining existing, and preferably on acquiring new, powerful friends.

Pressure must have been acute: after Sulla each year offered only two consulships, yet each created eight praetors eager to go on to occupy them. The scope for a less than wholly impartial administration of justice is obvious.

It may be that matters were worse in the provinces, although our evidence is thin. In Cicero's speeches against Verres we have an entire catalogue of the wrongdoing of a provincial governor, when exercising essentially the same control as a praetor over the grant or refusal of remedies (Cic., II *Verr.* 1.119–21; Frier 1985: 57–78).

The *lex Cornelia* therefore provides one early indication of a need to curb praetorian discretion. Another is provided by the presence in the edict of a curious clause translatable only awkwardly 'That he who has established a matter of law in relation to another person should be governed by the same law himself' (*quod quisque iuris in alterum statuerit, ut ipse eodem iure utatur*). A litigant who alleged that his adversary in court had, while himself a magistrate, made a particular decision could demand under this edict that the same decision be applied against him, and so require him to live by his own rule in his own case. The number of times it can have happened that a magistrate made a decision on the very point which then subsequently confronted him in his own case seems unlikely to have been very great, and the incentive to good behaviour provided by this edict correspondingly modest. None the less, the existence of this edict does seem to suggest that some effort may have been necessary to keep the magistrates in order (Lenel 1927: 58–9).

So far as municipal jurisdiction is concerned, it is likely that the same sorts of problems occurred. It is interesting that the municipal statutes not only provide what legal documents are to be displayed in the local forum but also take the trouble to spell out that they must be displayed 'so that they can be properly read from ground level' (*ut de plano recte legi possint*; *lex Irn.* ch. 85).

We can detect some institutional safeguards against abuse of their position by local magistrates. Chapter 84 of the *lex Irnitana* establishes a rather low limit on the jurisdiction of the local magistrates at Irni. In particular, as we have seen, any case in which condemnation would lead the defendant to suffer *infamia* could not be heard at Irni unless the defendant consented to it. Instead it must be remitted to the provincial governor. For a small community such as Irni it might well have been difficult for a defendant to obtain justice at the local level, if he happened to have alienated key figures in the administration of justice. It was therefore vital that he be entitled to insist on his case going before a court at some remove, where personal prejudice within the local community would play a much less significant role.

4. Could judges be relied upon?

The judges under the formulary system were not lawyers, but individuals selected by the parties to determine their dispute. They were there to get the answer to the (implied) questions in the formula right, by hearing the necessary evidence. Whether they succeeded in doing so is impossible to tell: it is obscured to a large degree by the 'yes or no' judgment, with absolutely no reasons, which the formulary system entailed; and by the fact that there was no appeal from the judge, so that we never hear of judges being put right by higher courts. Naturally, mistakes were made; and from time to time jurists speak of the ignorance or stupidity of judges; the same happens nowadays, of course (Ulpian, *D.* 21.2.51 pr.; Paul, *D.* 24.3.17.2). Where legal problems arose in relating the facts to the formula, the judge would require to call for legal advice. Judges tended to sit with a panel of advisers (*consilium*), at least one of whom might have had legal expertise. Although our evidence is late, it also seems that judges often sat with assessors, who are likely on the whole to have had legal knowledge with which they could assist the judge (Paul, *D.* 1.22.1). It is true that there is no guarantee that an assessor would be appointed on grounds of professional competence rather than personal favour. But this, and the additional possibility of consulting jurists, must have introduced at least an element of legal rigour into proceedings.

The second-century author Aulus Gellius in a well-known passage describes his difficulties on being appointed judge in a case. In the end, having taken advice, he was simply unable to reach a decision and took the only way out open to him: to swear an oath that he could not decide (*sibi non liquere*). That was one possibility, although the judge would be expected preferably to return a decision to absolve or condemn (*Noctes atticae* 14.2).

Judges then were not appointed for their legal knowledge. It might be hoped that they would be appointed for their fair-mindedness and independence of mind. Is that hope warranted? In the past, considerable pessimism has been expressed about their honesty and their openness to corruption (Kelly 1966: 31–68). But it is worth bearing in mind evidence on the selection of judges which has come to light since these negative assessments were made. For the first time, the *lex Irnitana* gives us full information about the criteria for eligibility to be a judge and the proce-

dure for selecting a judge in a given case. It is true that the *lex* relates to
municipal procedure, but there are strong reasons for thinking that it was
modelled on the procedure applicable in Rome itself. (See chapter 1
above and *lex Irn.* chs. 89, 91 and 93.)

The essential point is that the parties could agree on their own judge.
Only in the event of the parties' failure to agree on a name did the criteria in the *lex Irnitana* for eligibility to be a judge and the procedure for
appointment come into play. Chapter 86 requires that the magistrates
should within five days of entering office publish a list of those eligible
for appointment as judges, divided into three panels of equal size. The
number to be appointed is fixed by the provincial governor. The main
criteria are that the person should be a decurion or councillor, or otherwise be of free birth, over the age of twenty-five, and meet a certain
property qualification. (It seems likely that the property qualification
varied according to the municipality in question, so there is no reason to
think that the extremely modest qualification demanded at Irni – 5,000
sesterces – would apply in larger municipalities.) In addition, those who
were ill or over sixty-five were not to be appointed.

From chapter 87 of the *lex* we learn that, if the parties could agree on
a judge, it was open to them to have the praetor appoint him as judge in
the case. If they could not agree, there was a system for arriving at a
name from the published lists. First, starting with the plaintiff, each party
would reject one of the three panels. From the remaining panel, the
parties would then alternately reject a name until only one was left. If
the number of names in the panel was uneven, the plaintiff had the first
rejection; if it was even, the defendant did: so in either case the defendant had the right to make the final rejection. The rigorousness with
which the *lex* attempts to eliminate possible partiality of the judge is
striking.

If both parties trusted a given individual sufficiently to agree to him
as their judge, the chances are that as a rule he would not be open to
bribery by either. Of course, we cannot assess how often agreement
would have been reached. It seems likely that very often it would have
been necessary to go through the process for selection of a judge. Here
too our new evidence suggests that great care was taken to devise a
system under which one could have some confidence that the judge ultimately appointed was not *parti pris*. Of course, it must be the case that
some judges, once appointed and in a position to determine the outcome
of the case, would have seen this as an opportunity to earn some money.
There is no shortage of literary references to corrupt judges, and even

the jurists from time to time refer to the unfairness of judges (Ulpian, *D.* 3.6.1.3; *D.* 49.1.1 pr.). There were, however, procedures for replacing judges who had a conflict of interest: such as the one who was appointed heir by one of the litigants (Ulpian, *D.* 5.1.17).

There were other devices to attempt to keep the judge in order. There is, for example, an institution in Roman law known as the 'judge who makes the case his own' (*iudex qui litem suam facit*). This falls within the category of quasi-delicts, a rather miscellaneous category of civil wrongs which imposed liability in damages on the wrongdoer. The evidence on this is very meagre, although it has again been usefully supplemented by the *lex Irnitana*. It now seems that the judge was regarded as making the case his own, and therefore as becoming personally liable to satisfy the plaintiff's claim, if he exceeded his powers by failing to deliver a judgment, or validly adjourn proceedings, within the time provided for him; but also if his judgment was tainted by bad faith (*lex Irn.* ch. 91; Ulpian, *D.* 5.1.15.1).

So far as the *cognitio* procedure was concerned, much of what has been said above does not apply, since the parties did not select their own judge. Here they were effectively at the mercy of the magistrate, who decided that question for them. In essence, therefore, this comes back to the question whether the magistrate himself could be relied upon. To that, little can usefully be added to what was said above, other than to note that imperial guidance was given that it would be inappropriate to appoint as judge a person specifically requested by one of the parties (Callistratus, *D.* 5.1.47).

Yet matters go further than the legal knowledge and fairness of the judge: the question also arises how the judge would actually discharge his role. Since in formulary procedure the judges were not professional, there is a limit to what can usefully be said in general about judicial behaviour. So far as the evidence is concerned, there were established rules about which party bore the burden of proof: in broad terms, the plaintiff must prove the essence of his case, and the defendant the essence of any defence (Celsus, *D.* 22.3.13; Ulpian, *D.* 22.3.19 pr.; Kaser 1996: 363). Matters are vaguer when it comes to the witnesses and other evidence actually led in court. The material preserved in the Digest (*D.* 22.3) and Code (*C.* 4.19) is of limited value here, since nearly all of it appears to be concerned with the *cognitio* system of procedure.

There can be little doubt that the Roman judge might take into account factors which to a modern judge would seem irrelevant. Considerations about the relative worthiness and social status of the parties played an open part, greater (it is to be hoped) than they do today. The issue of worthiness is the first point mentioned by the jurist Callistratus in his remarks on weighing up the credibility of witnesses' testimony, and his approach is supported by the rescript of the emperor Hadrian which he goes on to quote (*D.* 22.5.3). (Although this is clearly a case of *cognitio*, the same seems likely to have applied in the formulary procedure too.) The same concern surfaces in Gellius' case: he was urged that his was a court of law not of morals, and his *consilium* of advisers took the view that he should absolve the defendant owing to lack of evidence, but a philosopher he consulted advised him to place more weight on the character of the parties involved (14.2.8–9, 21–3). The fact that insufficiency of evidence was not itself decisive for Gellius speaks volumes.

It is clear from the literary sources that 'evidence' was often produced to make an emotional impact, or because of the favourable light it cast upon a party in general terms, rather than because it was germane to the point at issue. Cicero's speeches, even in civil litigation, contain (by modern standards) extraordinary abuse of the defendant, his witnesses, and – this is barely an exaggeration – his relatives and friends. The same was true of litigation in Athens. It may be that running this gauntlet was a deterrent to some litigants (Kelly 1976: 97–8). It does, however, seem doubtful that this was absolutely standard practice for civil proceedings before a single judge, on whom such outpourings of rhetoric might well have been wasted. In the early second century AD Pliny implies that the place for real rhetorical flights was the centumviral court, where there was a much larger audience. As in Athens, the popular entertainment provided there must have been not least at the expense of the litigants and their good names.

Until Justinian's day, in the ordinary case no special importance seems to have been attached to written evidence, so the judge's assessment of the credibility and reliability of the witnesses must have been decisive (Scaevola, *D.* 22.3.29 pr.; Gel., 14.2.7; Kaser 1996: 369, 600; Peachin 1996: 70; Crook 1995: 144).

5. Representation in court

Although the legal sources say little about it, it seems that as a matter of course litigants would usually be represented by advocates, practitioners of rhetoric rather than law. This was quite the opposite of the position in Athens, where the rule was that the litigant would present his case in person, although this might just amount to delivering a speech composed by someone else, and it was also possible to enlist another person to make a supporting speech (Crook 1995: 30–4). But in Rome representation was normal in civil, as in criminal, and administrative cases. The evidence does not suggest that cost stood in the way of people getting advocates or that they were instructed purely by those of the highest social classes: the papyri indicate rather that advocates might appear even for parties of apparently modest means and in cases of modest significance (Crook 1995: 62–9, 131–5).

Nowadays the costs of litigation are high, and it is well known that there is a poverty trap: the rich can afford to litigate and so can those who are sufficiently badly off that they are eligible for legal aid from the state. The situation in Rome was different. There was no legal aid. But neither advocates nor jurists were paid. Instead, litigation meant undertaking social obligations, which might be called upon in the future; it meant entering upon the network of patron and client relationships. It would of course be naive to assume that justice was therefore open to everyone. The reality must have been that success in litigation depended on interesting the best possible jurist in giving advice, and the best possible advocate in presenting the case. In a way, such things are more easily managed if it is a simple matter of paying for them.

6. Other obstacles

Access to knowledge of the law must have been difficult for both litigants and judges, especially outside Rome and major provincial centres. The edict itself was a model of concision and precision rather than clarity. The writings of the jurists, if available, were alarmingly extensive: every edictal provision and more besides had been scrutinized and closely commented on in detail.

There were problems of legal certainty induced by the fact that the jurists conspicuously failed to agree on certain issues: the outcome of a case might turn on the chance of which jurist of which persuasion happened to be consulted by the judge. (On the other hand, much turns today too in British courts on the chance which judge is allocated to hear a particular case.)

From Pliny's experience in Bithynia it is clear that in the provinces access even to a basic library of legal materials could not be taken for granted. As the volume of imperial law-making grew, so did the problems of knowing where to find a given rescript; so even did the difficulties in knowing whether a rescript relied upon by one of the litigants was genuine (Plin., *ep.* 10.65–6; also *C.* 9.22.3 (AD 227)). These difficulties would not be resolved until systematic attempts were made to collect and order imperial rescripts. But this was not to happen until the end of the third century.

The massive edictal commentaries, especially those of Ulpian and Paul of the early third century, may have done something to satisfy this need for knowledge. Clear and comprehensive, authoritative, and in a sense consolidating the work of their predecessors in the two centuries before, these works may well have helped to fill the gap in knowledge about the law and the helplessness inspired by its immense volume.

7. Conclusions: the quality of justice

Litigation in Rome was fraught with more difficulty than the works of the Roman jurists may suggest. There were difficulties of access to knowledge about the law; difficulty in activating its procedures; doubts about the quality and impartiality of both magistrates and judges. To draw firm conclusions about the quality of justice in a system of this sort is literally impossible. But three final points may be made.

First, it is essential to remain constantly aware of the nature of our sources. To read modern books of law would not give a perfect picture of the realities of vindicating rights in practice. No more should we expect the writings of the Roman jurists to achieve that. A fuller picture requires the use of other kinds of sources.

Second, the Roman system – extraordinary and brilliant though the achievements of its jurists were – is not above criticism. Is that surprising? In any system run by humans, as the Roman one apparently was, there will be human error, and scope for human frailty and prejudice. The aim can only be to attempt to reduce these failings to proportions which are tolerable. In this chapter we have seen some of the safeguards which were introduced in the attempt to achieve precisely that. Of these perhaps the most notable is a general tendency towards centralization: if justice was hard to obtain in a local jurisdiction because of the lack of knowledge or competence or the prejudice of local magistrates, the solution lay in directing decision-making onward and upward. Under the formulary procedure, although there was no appeal, there was concern, attested by the municipal statutes, to direct important cases to regional or central jurisdictions. While this must have caused delay and expense, both of which might have been unwelcome and prejudicial, it must have done much to improve the quality of the administration of justice. Under the *cognitio* system, a system of appeals from lower magistrates to higher ones and finally to the emperor ought again to have given hope that justice would ultimately be achieved.

Third, it is vital to avoid the dangers of anachronism. Acceptable Roman law is law that was acceptable in Rome. Our own standards and expectations are plainly different. Although Roman judges undoubtedly could and did consider material which would be inadmissible in a modern court, in their judgments they embodied the values of their society. It is hard to claim that they should have done anything else.

Epilogue

The classical period of Roman law is conventionally taken to have ended in AD 235 with the death of the emperor Severus Alexander. It is true that the line of independent classical jurists breaks off there. But this was not a collapse but a change of direction. The leading jurists increasingly became involved in the process of imperial law-making; and their works were the constitutions they composed in the name of their emperor. The constitutions of Diocletian in particular (AD 284–305) show that half a century after the end of the classical period the standards of classical jurisprudence had been maintained. But this was not a period in which new original juristic work appeared; instead the trend was towards the production of anthologies or epitomes of leading classical works. It therefore seems appropriate to refer to the period from about AD 235 to 305 as the 'epiclassical' period of Roman law and to date the decisive break between the classical and the post-classical to about AD 300 (Wieacker 1971).

Yet the culmination of the classical tradition of Roman law was still to come. It came in the shape of the classical revival which took place during the reign of the emperor Justinian, and whose leading event was the compilation of the various parts of the *Corpus iuris civilis*. But by this time the western half of the Roman empire had long since fallen to barbarian invasion. Although during his reign Justinian succeeded in reconquering Italy as well as north Africa and Spain, these gains were soon reversed. The result was that Justinian's compilations never became firmly embedded in the West. Instead, nations of the West lived by the law codes promulgated by their Germanic kings: the Visigoths by the *lex Romana Visigothorum*, the Burgundians by the *lex Romana Burgundionum* and the Ostrogoths by the *Edictum Theoderici*. All of these codes drew heavily on Roman materials but their analytical level fell far short of that of the Justinianic compilations. The *Corpus iuris civilis* would remain unknown in the West for the next five centuries.

It is around 1100 that the study of Roman law appears to have revived, most likely owing to the import of the Digest, Code and Institutes from the East where they had never been lost. This revival is associated with the figure of Irnerius and with Bologna. Here begins what Vinogradoff described as a 'ghost story', 'a second life of Roman Law after the demise of the body in which it first saw the light'. Certainly, this is the story of a ghost doomed to walk for an exceptionally long time (Vinogradoff 1909: 4).

The impetus given to the study of law by the rediscovery of legal materials so rich, so substantial and so elaborate is almost impossible to exaggerate. There is no better way to illustrate this than to say a few words about the various schools of jurists of the following centuries, each of which adopted a very different approach to the Roman texts. (An illuminating account of all of them may be found in Wieacker 1995.)

First came the glossators, who from the twelfth century wrote marginal comments ('glosses'), explaining the texts and cross-referring to others. Their concern was to explain the texts using scholastic and logical methods. They were quite unconcerned with the practical application of the texts but treated them as a pure and timeless object of study.

The glossators were followed by the commentators, so called because of their more sustained commentaries on the Digest and Code, which began to appear in the course of the fourteenth century. The commentators did not confine themselves to the study of Roman law alone, and they attempted to accommodate the Roman texts to the demands of legal practice, even although this naturally involved construing the texts in a way quite different from what their ancient authors had intended.

As early as the fourteenth and fifteenth centuries the first signs of the third movement, of humanists, appear. With them came a backlash against the practical application of the Roman texts: the humanists' concern was to understand the classical signification of each text, and their contempt for what they saw as the crude efforts of their predecessors was undisguised. The quest for the classical also led the humanists to make the first attempts to separate out the elements in the Digest written by the classical Roman jurists and the words put into their mouths by Justinian: in short, the humanists were the first interpolation hunters.

In the seventeenth century the natural lawyers, Grotius and those who followed him, used the Roman texts in yet another way. For their purposes, the texts were not authoritative but they could still be called into service either as illustrations of the natural order of law or as rules of positive law to be compared with the rational tenets of natural law.

The Roman legal texts were therefore capable of inspiring quite divergent methodologies and conceptions about the nature of jurisprudence. But matters went further than this: it was not the least of the attractions of the Digest that it supplied a fund of texts to suit all tastes even in the sphere of political discourse. For instance, for debates about sovereignty the Digest could supply proponents of autocracy with the brocard that the emperor was not bound by statutes (*princeps legibus solutus est, D.* 1.3.31) and republicans with the proposition that he should profess himself to be subject to them (*digna vox maiestate regnantis legibus alligatum se principem profiteri, C.* 1.14.4).

Alongside all this scholarly activity it is important to remember too that the Roman texts represented positive law, applicable by the courts. It is true that Roman law was not the only law available: the Church began early to develop its own law, canon law, although this too was in parts substantially influenced by Roman law; local customs also played an important part; and feudal laws suppressed the Roman legal rules relating to land. None the less, there was an important residual role for Roman law to play right into the eighteenth century.

Roman legal concepts and institutions spread throughout Europe. It is often suggested that England was immune to these currents and remained in splendid isolation. But research is gradually redrawing this picture: although there is much work still to do, the relevance and the importance of the Roman-law tradition in England as early as the thirteenth century – and as late as the nineteenth century – have already begun to emerge (Helmholz 1990; Hoeflich 1997).

The Enlightenment represented a break with the old order, including unquestioning reliance upon Roman law. None the less, the law of reason did not cast aside all that had gone before. What it did demand was that law should be systematic and orderly, so as to serve the needs of society. This involved a preference for legislation and in particular for the codification of law. Of the earlier codes the most influential was the French Code civil of 1804, which applied not only in France but was imposed by Napoleon in the Netherlands, served as a model for Italy and Spain, and was adopted in Louisiana. Following these national codifications, it became inadmissible to rely on Roman law, since all the law was now contained in the code. While for this reason Roman law is now of no authority in countries which rely on national codes, the fruits of the Roman-law tradition are still clearly to be seen in codes such as the Code civil or the German Bürgerliches Gesetzbuch of 1900. On the other hand, in uncodified systems such as those of Scotland and South Africa, Roman law continues in the absence of clear modern authority to be persuasive and is cited in the courts from time to time.

Much of the earlier history of the western European tradition was therefore formed by the differing reactions to, and uses made of, the *Corpus iuris civilis* by successive generations of jurists. But this is not simply a matter of history: elements derived from the Roman-law tradition remain present not just in continental legal systems but even in the common law. The Roman-law tradition therefore represents a small area of common ground among the legal systems of western Europe. For this reason it has its part to play in current debate about the formation of a new private law for Europe (Zimmermann 1998). Quite apart from this, however, the Digest represents a fund of ideas and principles which is a vital resource even for modern legal systems (Johnston 1997b).

The main concern of this book has been the attempt to explore Roman law in the light of the society which created it. It may seem paradoxical that law developed for the needs of a specific ancient society should have been found sufficiently resilient to serve in societies quite remote and wholly disparate. Is this because Roman law is the best of laws for the best of all possible worlds? Perhaps. But a more likely explanation is this: the history of the Roman-law tradition is not a history of the fettering of later generations by the Roman legal texts. It is a history of their liberation, by responding to and building upon a system of jurisprudence of extraordinary sophistication.

Glossary of legal terms

This glossary is not exhaustive: it contains only a few terms of Roman law which are used on several occasions in this book and which it is convenient to define here rather than each time they occur. Further details and references can be found in A. Berger, *Encyclopedic Dictionary of Roman Law* (1953); here reference is made (in brackets) only to relevant passages, if any, in the Institutes of Gaius.

actio: a legal action, a claim or suit brought by a plaintiff (4.1–4); an action *in personam* asserted a claim against a person, for example under a contract; an action *in rem* a claim for a thing

bonae fidei iudicia: a legal action in which the judge was given discretion to determine the case according to the standard of good faith; the converse was the action *stricti iuris*, in which the judge enjoyed no such discretion (4.61–2)

cautio: a promise or undertaking, made by *stipulatio*; the term also denotes a written document which was evidence of the promise

cognitio: a late form of civil procedure in which an official was responsible for the conduct of the entire procedure; by contrast, in formulary procedure the phase of proceedings during which evidence was led was held before a private individual (*iudex*)

condictio: an action *in personam* asserting that the defendant was under an obligation to give something to, or do something for, the plaintiff; in classical law this was available only for claims for specific sums or objects (4.5)

damnum infectum: damage 'not done' but threatened by the ruinous state of a neighbour's property; the praetor provided various remedies to encourage repair and against the event that the damage materialized

dominium: ownership

emptio venditio: contract of sale (3.139–41)

exceptio: a defence to the plaintiff's legal action, introducing a ground on which the defendant should not be condemned in the action (4.115–29)

fiducia: an agreement made in connexion with a conveyance of property; in particular, a type of security by which the debtor conveyed property in security to his creditor, the *fiducia* being the creditor's undertaking to convey it back again on satisfaction of the debt (2.60)

formula: in formulary procedure a statement issued by the praetor which appointed a judge, set out the legal issues raised by each of the parties, and gave the judge authority, having considered them, to determine whether the defendant should be absolved or condemned

institor: a person appointed by the owner of a business as its manager; the praetor made an action available directly against the owner of the business to those who dealt with the *institor* in the course of the business (4.71)

iudex: a judge in civil proceedings, responsible in formulary procedure for hearing evidence and deciding whether the defendant should be absolved or condemned in terms of the formula

locatio conductio: the contract of hire or letting, whether of a thing, of services or of a task to be done (3.142–7)

mancipatio: a formal conveyance in which, before five witnesses and a person holding a scale, ownership was conveyed 'by bronze and scale' to the acquirer; one of two possible methods for transferring ownership in *res mancipi*, the other being *in iure cessio* (1.119–22)

mutuum: loan of money or other consumables, concluded by delivery to the borrower (3.90)

peculium: a fund of property entrusted to a slave or to a child in the power of a paterfamilias, but which none the less remained the property of the paterfamilias; the praetor granted actions directly against the paterfamilias to those who had dealt with the slave or child, but such actions were limited in quantum to the value of the *peculium* (4.72a–74a)

pignus: a type of pledge which gave the pledge-creditor possession of the object pledged

possessio: physical control of, rather than entitlement to, an object, and so to be clearly distinguished from ownership; the possessor was protected by interdict

res mancipi: a thing the ownership of which required to be transferred by formal conveyance, *mancipatio* or *in iure cessio*, namely land, slaves, certain animals – such as oxen, horses, mules and asses, but not elephants or camels; all other items were *res nec mancipi* (1.120, 2.14a–23)

stipulatio: a contract entered into orally by formal exchange of corresponding question and answer (3.92)

sui heredes: heirs who were in the power of the paterfamilias at his death (2.156–7)

sui iuris: independent, not subject to paternal power

traditio: a means of conveyance by delivery, sufficient to transfer ownership in things which were not *res mancipi* (2.19)

usucapio: acquisition of ownership of a thing by possessing it for two years (for land) or one year (for anything else), provided the possession was begun in good faith, for a good cause and was of an object which had not been stolen (2.42–58)

ususfructus: a right to make use of and enjoy the fruits of the property of another person without impairing its substance

vindicatio: a legal action seeking recovery of property (4.5)

Bibliographical essay

It may be useful to begin with a note on the main modern works of reference and periodicals as well as the main ancient sources. The standard abbreviations used for them are also noted here.

TEXTBOOKS ON ROMAN LAW

For a basic account of the main institutions of Roman law, B. Nicholas, *An Introduction to Roman Law* (1962) is clear, elegant and valuable. For detailed information, resort to one of the larger textbooks will be necessary. The leading modern account is that of M. Kaser, *Das römische Privatrecht* (1971–5). In English the leading textbook is by W. W. Buckland, *A Textbook on Roman Law* (1963), a shade dry but exceptionally reliable and accurate; an alternative is J. A. C. Thomas, *Textbook on Roman Law* (1976). H. F. Jolowicz and B. Nicholas, *Historical Introduction to the Study of Roman Law* (1972), approaches the subject historically, and for a historian is probably a good place to start. F. Schulz, *Classical Roman Law* (1951) is a work by a great scholar which is sometimes idiosyncratic, often provocative but always interesting. The leading account of Roman law in its social context remains J. A. Crook, *Law and Life of Rome* (1967).

A. Berger, *Encyclopedic Dictionary of Roman Law* (1953) gives convenient brief entries on Roman legal terms and concepts.

OTHER GENERAL WORKS

F. Schulz, *Principles of Roman Law* (1936) attempts from the mass of Roman legal institutions to distil the essence, and has interesting chapters on such things as abstraction, tradition, fidelity and security. D. Daube, *Roman Law: Linguistic, Social and Philosophical Aspects* (1969) is a *tour de force*, full of remarkable insights, although not all have been shared by other scholars.

PERIODICALS

Periodical inflation means that only a few titles can be mentioned here. Leading journals, together with their usual abbreviations, are: *Zeitschrift der Savigny-Stiftung für Rechtsgeschichte (Romanistische Abteilung) (SZ or ZSS)* (Weimar); *Tijdschrift voor Rechtsgeschiedenis (TR)* (Haarlem), *Studia et documenta historiae et iuris (SDHI)*

(Rome*)*, *Bullettino del istituto di diritto romano (BIDR)* (Rome), *Revue internationale des droits de l'antiquité (RIDA)* (Brussels); *Revue historique de droit français et étranger (RHD)* (Paris). The journals *Labeo* (Naples) and *IURA* (Naples) contain in addition useful annual bibliographies of publications on Roman law and related subjects. A bibliography is also published by the Institut de droit romain in Paris.

Some useful sources and materials can be accessed on or via a website maintained at Aberdeen University: http://www.abdn.ac.uk/~law113/rl/sites.htmi

SOURCES

The edition of the *Corpus iuris civilis* most commonly used is the so-called stereotype edition (frequently reprinted), volume 1 of which contains the Institutes and Digest, edited by P. Krueger and Th. Mommsen; volume 2 contains the Code, edited by P. Krueger; and volume 3 the Novels, edited by R. Schoell and W. Kroll. There is an *editio maior* of the Digest by Th. Mommsen, *Digesta Iustiniani Augusti* (1870) with a preface containing valuable information on the textual tradition of the Digest. The *editio maior* of Justinian's Code is by P. Krueger, *Codex Iustinianus* (1877).

There are many editions of Gaius's Institutes. A reliable one is by B. Kübler and E. Seckel in the Teubner series. The principal critical edition with commentary is by M. David and H. Nelson, continued by M. David and U. Manthe, *Gaii Institutionum commentarii quattuor.* This started in 1954 and after a long gap the latest volume appeared in 1992, taking it up to book 3.87. An *editio minor* based on this critical edition has already appeared (1964).

The texts of most Roman statutes attested epigraphically are given in volume 1 of S. Riccobono et al., *Fontes iuris romani anteiustiniani (FIRA)* (1940–3, new edn 1968–9). They also appear with commentary in M. Crawford, ed., *Roman Statutes* (1996), together with statutes attested by literary sources. A summary of the content of all Roman statutes is given in G. Rotondi, *Leges publicae populi Romani* (reprint, 1962); a new edition is in progress.

FIRA is also a convenient source for some of the works of classical jurists predating the Digest (vol. 2) and legal documents such as inscriptions and papyri (vol. 3). Other documents of legal practice are published in G. Camodeca, *L'archivio puteolano dei Sulpicii* I (1992) and discussed by J. G. Wolf in a series of publications: see Wolf 1985 and Wolf and Crook 1989 in the bibliography, both with further references. The Herculaneum tablets are conventionally abbreviated as TH; the Pompeian ones as TP (although Camodeca uses the form TP Sulp for those he discusses). N. Lewis, Y. Yadin and J. C. Greenfield, *The Documents from the Bar Kokhba Period in the Cave of Letters* (1989) publish the papyri from the archive of Babatha, ranging from the first to second century AD.

TRANSLATIONS

A. Watson, ed., *The Digest of Justinian* (1985) prints a translation opposite the text of Mommsen's *editio maior.* The translation is the work of many different translators and is for that reason uneven, but it is the best version available in English. Corrections and comments on it are posted on a website: http://www.abdn.ac.uk/~law113/rl/dig/dg_main.htmi. A more reliable translation, into German, is the continuing version by O. Behrends et al., *Corpus iuris civilis: Text und Übersetzung* (Heidelberg, 1990–). So far this has covered Justinian's Institutes and reached book 10 of the Digest. English translations of the Institutes of Gaius are provided by F. de Zulueta, *The Institutes of Gaius* (1946) with commentary (1953), and W. M. Gordon and O. F. Robinson, *The Institutes of Gaius* (1988). Recent translations of Justinian's Institutes are by J. A. C. Thomas, *The Institutes of Justinian* (1975) with commentary, and P. Birks and G. McLeod, *The Institutes of Justinian* (1987), the accompanying commentary on which is E. Metzger, ed., *A Companion to Justinian's Institutes* (1998).

CHAPTER 1: INTRODUCTION

Extensive general accounts of the sources of Roman law are given in H. F. Jolowicz and B. Nicholas, *Historical Introduction to the Study of Roman Law* (1972) and A. A. Schiller, *Roman Law: Mechanisms of Development* (1978). F. Wieacker, *Römische Rechtsgeschichte* I (1988) gives a magisterial introduction to use of the sources followed by an account of Roman legal history until the end of the republic. Volume II (to appear posthumously) will cover the principate, but unfortunately without the rich apparatus of notes provided in volume I.

On the jurists in particular, F. Schulz, *History of Roman Legal Science* (1946) remains indispensable. W. Kunkel, *Herkunft und soziale Stellung der römischen Juristen* (1967) reconstructs biographies of the individual jurists so far as possible. Recent work on the schools of jurists is to be found in G. L. Falchi, *Le controversie tra sabiniani e proculiani* (1981) as well as in the papers by Stein (1972) and Liebs (1976) referred to in the bibliography. A. M. Honoré gives fascinating accounts of the work of individual jurists in *Gaius* (1962) and *Ulpian* (1982), although the method – analysing the jurist's Latin style – on which they are based is controversial. A substantial number of monographs on individual juristic works has appeared from the Freiburg school under Professor J. G. Wolf; recent highlights include the works by B. Eckardt (1978), U. Manthe (1982) and J. Schmidt-Ott (1993) listed in the bibliography; others can be found in the series Freiburger rechtsgeschichtliche Abhandlungen. Some useful essays on individual jurists are contained in the world's largest Festschrift (for J. Vogt), *Aufstieg und Niedergang der römischen Welt* vol. II 15 (1976).

On the emperor, F. Millar, *The Emperor in the Roman World* (1977) provides a detailed general account; A. M. Honoré, *Emperors and Lawyers* (1994), although mainly concerned with dating the tenure of different secretaries *a libellis*, gives an admirable survey of the rescript system in chs. 1–2.

ROME AND THE PROVINCES

The classic work is L. Mitteis, *Reichsrecht und Volksrecht in den östlichen Provinzen des römischen Kaiserreichs* (1891). Since then a remarkable amount of interesting material has been discovered. A modern account of the essentials is in A. Lintott, *Imperium Romanum: politics and administration* (1993). On municipal administration in the light of the *lex Irnitana*, F. Lamberti, *Tabulae irnitanae: municipalità e ius romanorum* (1993) is a useful guide, not least to further literature, while the article by Wolff (1980) cited in the bibliography covers the eastern, non-municipal side.

CHAPTER 2: SOURCES AND METHODOLOGY

F. Wieacker's *Römische Rechtsgeschichte*, already mentioned, is the best modern account on use of the sources. Two classic works are H. Kantorowicz, *Einführung in die Textkritik* (1911), concerned (as the title suggests) with textual critical questions, and F. Schulz, *Einführung in das Studium der Digesten* (1916), which provides a more general account.

O. Lenel, *Palingenesia iuris civilis* (1889) reconstructs the works of the classical jurists from the fragments contained in the Digest and so makes it possible to consider them in their original context. This work and Lenel's *Das Edictum perpetuum* (see below) are the fundamental works of modern Romanistic scholarship. Lenel's work has been modified in details, but remains essential. A useful critical review of it is given by Th. Kipp (1891); two recent articles which deal with modifications to Lenel's work are those by H. Ankum (1994) and D. Johnston (1997a); an exemplary demonstration of what can be achieved with the palingenetic method is given in D. Daube (1959): for details of all of these see the bibliography.

On interpolation in the Digest, there is a massive literature. The modern conservative tendency is outlined in M. Kaser, *Zur Methode der römischen Rechtsquellenforschung* (1972). A more radical approach was followed by F. Wieacker, whose views are now conveniently summarized in his *Römische Rechtsgeschichte*. In English, a recent brief discussion with further references is in D. Johnston (1989): see the bibliography.

CHAPTER 3: FAMILY AND INHERITANCE

R. Saller, *Patriarchy, Property and Death in the Roman Family* (1994) sets out the demographic context in which the Roman family should be viewed, with much attention to the legal sources. This provides a major corrective to earlier views about the structure of the Roman family. It also contains references to the very extensive literature in this area. K. Hopkins, *Death and Renewal* (1983) is important in setting the law of succession in similar perspective. S. Treggiari, *Roman Marriage* (1991) is a rich discussion of marriage in the light of literary and legal sources. M. Humbert, *Le remariage à Rome* (1972) is a major work on the impact on the law of the fact that many Roman marriages were of brief duration; some of his conclusions have now to be modified in the light of Treggiari's work.

On slaves, the classic work is W. W. Buckland, *The Roman Law of Slavery* (1908), which goes into great detail on virtually every conceivable question. A very brief account is in A. Watson, *Roman Slave Law* (1987). A short and valuable historical treatment may be found in K. Bradley, *Slavery and Society at Rome* (1994).

On the law of succession, the standard modern treatise is P. Voci, *Diritto ereditario romano* (1963–7). M. Amelotti, *Il testamento romano* (1966) is an important treatment of Roman wills in the light of documentary evidence. F. von Woess, *Das römische Erbrecht und die Erbanwärter* (1911) is a marvellous work, well in advance of its time, which sets the law of succession in its context; though difficult to find, it is well worth seeking out. A more recent and rather successful work with a similar aim is E. Champlin, *Final Judgments* (1991). D. Johnston, *The Roman Law of Trusts* (1988) is mainly an account of the development of the law relating to *fideicommissa* but attempts to place this against the background of the evolution of the law of succession and (to some extent) social history in general. An important article by L. Boyer (1965) discusses legacies in their social context: see the bibliography.

CHAPTER 4: PROPERTY

On the use of land, B. W. Frier, *Landlords and Tenants in Imperial Rome* (1980) is a pioneering work which explores the law of urban leases with full reference to literary and archaeological evidence. D. Kehoe, *Investment Profit and Tenancy: the Jurists and the Roman Agrarian Economy* (1997) attempts a similar sort of exercise for rural leases.

On relations with neighbours, A. Rodger, *Owners and Neighbours in Roman Law* (1972) is a fundamental treatment especially of urban servitudes. J. M. Rainer, *Bau- und nachbarrechtliche Bestimmungen im klassischen römischen Recht* (1987) covers the wider range of remedies relevant to relations with neighbours.

CHAPTER 5: COMMERCE

An excellent, interesting, and readable account of the law of contract in general (and much more besides) is given in R. Zimmermann, *The Law of Obligations* (1990). For discussion of virtually any topic raised in this chapter, this is the best place to start, and there is therefore no need to give further references here on sale or on lending.

The major work on banking is J. Andreau, *La vie financière dans le monde romain* (1987); a briefer account by the same author is his *Banking and Business in the Roman World* (1999). From a more legal point of view, the article by Bürge (1987: see the bibliography) is also important; his criticism of the extent to which it makes sense to speak of banking in ancient Rome requires modification in the light of Andreau's work. P. Gröschler, *Die Tabellae-Urkunden aus den pompejanischen und herkulanensischen Urkundenfunden* (1997) analyses some of the surviving documents dealing with bankers.

S. Martin, *The Roman Jurists and the Organization of Private Building in the Late Republic and Early Empire* (1989) provides a clear and comprehensive account of the workings of building contracts, making full use of legal and literary evidence.

Agents have had a good deal of recent attention in useful works by A. Kirschenbaum, *Sons, Slaves and Freedmen in Roman Commerce* (1987), and particularly A. di Porto, *Impresa collettiva e schiavo manager in Roma antica* (1984) and J.-J. Aubert, *Business Managers in Ancient Rome: a Social and Economic Study of Institores 200 BC – AD 250* (1994). From a more purely legal point of view, the article in the bibliography by A. Wacke (1994) is also worth consulting.

CHAPTER 6: LITIGATION

M. Kaser, *Das römische Zivilprozessrecht* (1996) is the leading modern account of the workings of Roman civil procedure and contains substantial bibliography. O. Lenel, *Das Edictum perpetuum* (1927) reconstructs the praetor's edict, together with the formula for each action. This work laid the basis for much of modern Romanistic scholarship and, while it has been refined in details, it remains unsurpassed.

On the social context of Roman litigation, there are two books by J. M. Kelly, *Roman Litigation* (1966), and *Studies in the Civil Judicature of the Roman Republic* (1976), both interesting, the first very (perhaps excessively) critical of the extent to which Roman litigation was fair. Similar issues are discussed for the principate in P. Garnsey, *Social Status and Legal Privilege in the Roman Empire* (1970).

B. W. Frier, *The Rise of the Roman Jurists* (1985) gives a wonderfully rich account of Roman civil litigation based on Cicero's *pro Caecina*. J. A. Crook, *Legal Advocacy in the Roman World* (1995) adds another dimension to discussions of litigation by insisting on the continuing importance of the advocate. M. Peachin, *Iudex vice Caesaris* (1996), although his concern is primarily with emperors and those who deputized for them in administering justice, gives a useful account of litigation under the principate.

Provincial and municipal jurisdictions have become rather fashionable since the discovery of the *lex Irnitana*. References to the massive bibliography, a reliable text and some useful commentary are contained in F. Lamberti, *Tabulae irnitanae: municipalità e ius romanorum* (1993).

EPILOGUE

Useful short treatments of the later life of Roman law are given in R. van Caenegem, *An Historical Introduction to Private Law* (1992) and P. Stein, *Roman Law in European History* (1999). Rich and fascinating, detailed accounts may be found in P. Koschaker, *Europa and das römische Recht* (1947), J. P. Dawson, *The Oracles of the Law* (1968) and F. Wieacker, *A History of Private Law in Europe* (1995).

Bibliography

AMELOTTI, M. (1966) *Il testamento romano*. Florence

ANDREAU, J. (1987) *La vie financière dans le monde romain*. Rome
(1999) *Banking and Business in the Roman World*. Cambridge

ANKUM, H. (1994) 'Towards additions to Lenel's *Palingenesia iuris civilis*', *RIDA* 41: 125–38

AUBERT, J.-J. (1994) *Business Managers in Ancient Rome: a Social and Economic Study of Institores 200 BC–AD 250*. Leiden – New York

BLUHME, F. (1820) 'Die Ordnung der Fragmente in den Pandectentiteln', *Zeitschrift für Rechtsgeschichte* 4 = *Labeo* 6: 50–96, 235–77, 368–404 (1960)

BONFANTE, P. (1926) *Corso di diritto romano* II: *La proprietà*. 2 vols. Rome

BOYER, L. (1965) 'La fonction sociale des legs d'après la jurisprudence classique', *RHD* 43: 333–408

BRADLEY, K. (1994) *Slavery and Society at Rome*. Cambridge

BUCKLAND, W. W. (1908) *The Roman Law of Slavery*. Cambridge, repr. 1968
(1963) *A Textbook of Roman Law*. 3rd edn, rev. P. Stein. Cambridge

BÜRGE, A. (1987) 'Fiktion und Wirklichkeit: soziale und rechtliche Strukturen des römischen Bankwesens', *SZ* 104: 465–558

CAMODECA, G. (1992) *L'archivio puteolano dei Sulpicii* I. Naples

CHAMPLIN, E. (1991) *Final Judgments: Duty and Emotion in Roman Wills 200 BC to AD 250*. Berkeley

CHERRY, D. (1996) 'Intestacy and the Roman poor', *TR* 64: 155–72

CHIUSI, T. (1994) 'Zur Vormundschaft der Mutter', *SZ* 111: 155–96

COTTON, H. (1993) 'The guardianship of Jesus son of Babatha: Roman and local law in the province of Arabia', *JRS* 83, 94–108

CROOK, J. A. (1967) *Law and Life of Rome*. London – Ithaca
(1973) 'Intestacy in Roman society', *PCPS* 19: 38–44
(1986a) 'Women in Roman succession', in Rawson, B. M., ed., *The Family in Ancient Rome: New Perspectives*, 53–82. London
(1986b), 'Feminine inadequacy and the *SC Velleianum*', in Rawson, B. M., ed., *The Family in Ancient Rome: New Perspectives*, 83–92. London
(1995) *Legal Advocacy in the Roman World*. London

DAUBE, D. (1959) 'Zur Palingenesie einiger Klassikerfragmente', *SZ* 76: 149–264
(1965) 'The preponderance of intestacy at Rome', *Tulane Law Review* 39: 253–62

(1969) *Roman Law: Linguistic, Social and Philosophical Aspects*. Edinburgh

DAWSON, J. P. (1968) *The Oracles of the Law*. Ann Arbor

DUNCAN-JONES, R. P. (1982) *The Economy of the Roman Empire. Quantitative Studies*. 2nd edn. Cambridge

(1990) *Structure and Scale in the Roman Empire*. Cambridge

(1994) *Money and Government in the Roman Empire*. Cambridge

ECKARDT, B. (1978) *Iavoleni epistulae*. Berlin

ERNST, W. (1996) 'Gattungskauf und Lieferungskauf im römischen Recht', *SZ* 114: 272–344

FALCHI, G. L. (1981) *Le controversie tra sabiniani e proculiani*. Milan

FINLEY, M. I. (1976) 'Private farm tenancy in Italy before Diocletian', in Finley, M. I., ed., *Studies in Roman Property*, 103–21. Cambridge

FRIER, B. W. (1980) *Landlords and Tenants in Imperial Rome*. Princeton

(1982) 'Roman life-expectancy: Ulpian's evidence', *HSCP* 86: 212–51

(1985) *The Rise of the Roman Jurists*. Princeton

(1989–90) 'Law, economics and disasters down on the farm: *remissio mercedis* revisited', *BIDR* 31–2: 237–70

GARDNER, J. (1986) *Women in Roman Law and Society*. London

(1991) *Being a Roman Citizen*. London

(1998) *Family and familia in Roman Law and Life*. Oxford

GARNSEY, P. (1970) *Social Status and Legal Privilege in the Roman Empire*. Oxford

ed., (1980) *Non-Slave Labour in the Greco-Roman World*. Cambridge

GARNSEY, P. AND SALLER, R. P. (1987) *The Roman Empire: Economy, Society and Culture*. London

GRÖSCHLER, P. (1997) *Die tabellae-Urkunden aus den pompejanischen und herkulanensischen Urkundenfunden*. Berlin

HELMHOLZ, R. H. (1990) 'Continental law and common law: historical strangers or companions?', *Duke Law Journal* 1207–28

HOEFLICH, M. (1997) *Roman and Civil Law and the Development of Anglo-American Jurisprudence in the Nineteenth Century*. Athens, Georgia

HONORÉ, A. M. (1962) *Gaius*. Oxford

(1981) 'Some suggestions for the study of interpolations', *TR* 49: 225–49

(1982) *Ulpian*. Oxford

(1994) *Emperors and Lawyers*. 2nd edn. Oxford

HOPKINS, K. (1983) *Death and Renewal*. Cambridge

HUMBERT, M. (1972) *Le remariage à Rome. Etude d'histoire juridique et sociale*. Milan

JOHNSTON, D. (1988) *The Roman Law of Trusts*. Oxford

(1989) 'Justinian's Digest: the interpretation of interpolation', *Oxford Journal of Legal Studies* 9: 149–66

(1997a) 'Lenel's *Palingenesia iuris civilis*: four questions and an answer', *TR* 65: 57–70

(1997b) 'The renewal of the old', *Cambridge Law Journal* 56: 80–95

JOLOWICZ, H. F. and NICHOLAS, B. (1972) *Historical Introduction to the Study of Roman Law*. 3rd edn, rev. B. Nicholas. Cambridge

KALB, W. (1890) *Roms Juristen nach ihrer Sprache dargestellt*. Leipzig

KANTOROWICZ, H. (1911) *Einführung in die Textkritik*. Leipzig

KASER, M. (1971, 1975) *Das römische Privatrecht*. 2 vols. Munich
  (1972) *Zur Methode der römischen Rechtsquellenforschung*. Vienna
  (1996) *Das römische Zivilprozessrecht*. 2nd edn, rev. K. Hackl. Munich

KEHOE, D. (1997) *Investment, Profit and Tenancy: the Jurists and the Roman Agrarian Economy*. Ann Arbor

KELLY, J. M. (1966) *Roman Litigation*. Oxford
  (1976) *Studies in the Civil Judicature of the Roman Republic*. Oxford
  (1992) *A Short History of Western Legal Theory*. Oxford

KIPP, TH. (1891) 'Quellenkunde', *Kritische Vierteljahresschrift für Gesetzgebung und Rechtswissenschaft* 14: 481–580

KIRSCHENBAUM, A. (1987) *Sons, Slaves and Freedmen in Roman Commerce*. Jerusalem

KONSTAN, D. (1997) *Friendship in the Classical World*. Cambridge

KOSCHAKER, P. (1947) *Europa und das römische Recht*. Munich, repr. 1966

KUNKEL, W. (1967) *Herkunft und soziale Stellung der römischen Juristen*. 2nd edn. Graz–Vienna–Cologne

LAMBERTI, F. (1993) *Tabulae irnitanae: municipalità e ius romanorum*. Naples

LENEL, O. (1889) *Palingenesia iuris civilis*. 2 vols. Leipzig
  (1927) *Das Edictum perpetuum*. 3rd edn. Leipzig

LEWIS, N., YADIN, Y. and GREENFIELD, J. C. (1989) *The Documents from the Bar Kokhba Period in the Cave of Letters*. Jerusalem

LIEBS, D. (1976) 'Rechtsschulen und Rechtsunterricht im Prinzipat', in Temporini, H., ed., *Aufstieg und Niedergang der römischen Welt*, II 15, 197–286. Berlin
  (1987) *Die Jurisprudenz im spätantiken Italien*. Berlin
  (1993) *Römische Jurisprudenz in Africa*. Berlin

LINTOTT, A. (1993) *Imperium Romanum: Politics and Administration*. London

MANTHE, U. (1982) *Die libri ex Cassio des Iavolenus Priscus*. Berlin

MANTOVANI, D. (1987) *Digesto e masse Bluhmiane*. Milan

MARTIN, S. (1989) *The Roman Jurists and the Organization of Private Building in the Late Republic and Early Empire*. Brussels

METZGER, E. (1997) *A New Outline of the Roman Civil Trial*. Oxford
  ed., (1998) *A Companion to Justinian's Institutes*. London – Ithaca

MILLAR, F. (1977) *The Emperor in the Roman World*. London, repr. with afterword 1992

MILLETT, P. (1983) 'Maritime loans and the structure of credit in fourth-century Athens', in Garnsey, P., Hopkins, K., and Whittaker, C. R., eds., *Trade in the Ancient Economy*, 36–52. London
  (1990) 'Sale, credit and exchange in Athenian law and society', in Cartledge, P., Millett, P., and Todd, S., eds., *Nomos: Essays in Athenian Law Politics and Society*, 167–94. Cambridge
  (1991) *Lending and Borrowing in Ancient Athens*. Cambridge

MITTEIS, L. (1891) *Reichsrecht und Volksrecht in den ostlichen Provinzen des römischen Kaiserreichs*. Leipzig

MODRZEJEWSKI, J. (1970) 'La règle de droit dans l'Egypte romaine', *Proceedings of the XIIth International Congress of Papyrology*, 317–77. Toronto

NEEVE, P. W. DE (1983) '*Remissio mercedis*', *SZ* 100: 296–339
(1984) *Colonus*. Amsterdam

NICHOLAS, B. (1962) *An Introduction to Roman Law*. Oxford

NÖRR, D. (1998) 'Römisches Zivilprozessrecht nach Max Kaser', *SZ* 115: 80–98

PAKTER, W. (1994) 'The mystery of *cessio bonorum*', *Index* 22: 323–42

PAULUS, C. (1992) *Die Idee der postmortalen Persönlichkeit im römischen Testamentsrecht*. Berlin
(1994) 'Die Verrechtlichung der Familienbeziehungen in der Zeit der entgehenden Republik und ihr Einfluss auf die Testierfreiheit', *SZ* 111: 425–35

PEACHIN, M. (1996) *Iudex vice Caesaris*. Stuttgart

PORTO, A. DI (1984) *Impresa collettiva e schiavo manager in Roma antica*. Milan

PUGLIESE, G. (1957) 'In tema di *actio exercitoria*', *Labeo* 3: 308–43

RAINER, J. M. (1987) *Bau- und nachbarrechtliche Bestimmungen im klassischen römischen Recht*. Graz

RAWSON, B. M. ed., (1986) *The Family in Ancient Rome: New Perspectives*. London

ROBINSON, O. (1997) *The Sources of Roman Law*. London

RODGER, A. (1972) *Owners and Neighbours in Roman Law*. Oxford

SAINTE CROIX, G. E. M. DE (1974) 'Ancient Greek and Roman maritime loans', in Edey, H. and Yamey, B. S., eds., *Debits, Credits, Finance, and Profits: Studies in Honour of W. T. Baxter*, 41–59. London

SALLER, R. P. (1994) *Patriarchy, Property and Death in the Roman Family*. Cambridge

SCHILLER, A. A. (1978) *Roman Law: Mechanisms of Development*. New York

SCHMIDT-OTT, J. (1993) *Pauli quaestiones: Eigenart und Textgeschichte einer spätklassischen Juristenschrift*. Berlin

SCHULZ, F. (1916) *Einführung in das Studium der Digesten*. Tübingen
(1936) *Principles of Roman Law*. Oxford
(1946) *History of Roman Legal Science*. Oxford
(1951) *Classical Roman Law*. Oxford

SEALEY, R. (1994) *The Justice of the Greeks*. Ann Arbor

STEIN, P. (1972) 'The two schools of jurists in the early Roman principate', *Cambridge Law Journal* 31: 8–31
(1990) 'The origins of *stellionatus*', *IURA* 41: 79–89
(1999) *Roman Law in European History*. Cambridge

TALBERT, R. J. A. (1984) *The Senate of Imperial Rome*. Princeton

THOMAS, J. A. C. (1976) *Textbook on Roman Law*. Cape Town

TODD, S. C. (1993) *The Shape of Athenian Law* Oxford

TREGGIARI, S. (1991). *Roman Marriage*. Oxford

TURPIN, W. (1985) 'The law codes and late Roman law', *RIDA* 32: 339–53
(1987) 'The purpose of the Roman law codes', *SZ* 104: 620–30

VAN CAENEGEM. R. C. (1992) *An Historical Introduction to Private Law*. Cambridge, translated by D. Johnston

VINOGRADOFF, P. (1909) *Roman Law in Medieval Europe*. London, repr. 1968

VOCI, P. (1963, 1967) *Diritto ereditario romano.* 2 vols. (2nd edn of vol. 1 only). Milan

WACKE, A. (1994) 'Die adjektizischen Klagen im Überblick. Erster Teil: Von der Reeder- und Betriebsleiterklagen zur direkten Stellvertretung', *SZ* 111: 280–362

WALLACE-HADRILL, A. (1994) *Houses and Society in Pompeii and Herculaneum.* Princeton

WATSON, A. (1987) *Roman Slave Law.* Baltimore

(1994) 'Prolegomena to establishing pre-Justinianic texts', *TR* 62: 113–25

WEAVER, P. (1997) 'Children of Junian Latins', in Rawson, B. and Weaver, P., eds., *The Roman Family in Italy*, 55–73. Oxford

WHITTAKER, C. R. (1993) 'Trade and the aristocracy in the Roman Empire' in Whittaker, C. R., *Land, City and Trade in the Roman Empire*, 49–65. Aldershot

WIEACKER, F. (1971) 'Le droit romain de la mort d'Alexandre Sevère à l'avènement de Dioclétien (235–284 apr. J.-C.)', *RHD* 49: 201–23

(1988) *Römische Rechtsgeschichte I.* Munich

(1995) *A History of Private Law in Europe.* Oxford, translated by Tony Weir

WOESS, F. VON (1911) *Das römische Erbrecht und die Erbanwärter.* Berlin

WOLFF, H. J. (1980) 'Römisches Provinzialrecht in der Provinz Arabia', in Temporini, H., ed., *Aufstieg und Niedergang der römischen Welt*, II 13, 763–806. Berlin

WOLF, J. G. (1985) 'Das sogenannte Ladungsvadimonium', in Ankum, J. A. et al., eds., *Satura Roberto Feenstra oblata*, 59–69. Fribourg

(1994) 'Claudius iudex', in Strocka, V. M., ed., *Die Regierungszeit des Kaisers Claudius (41–54 n. Chr.)*, 145–58. Mainz

WOLF, J. G. and CROOK, J. A. (1989) *Rechtsurkunden in Vulgarlatein aus den Jahren 37–39 n. Chr.* Heidelberg

ZIMMERMANN, R. (1990) *The Law of Obligations. Roman Foundations of the Civilian Tradition.* Cape Town

(1998) 'Roman law and European legal unity', in Hartkamp, A. et al., eds., *Towards a European Civil Code*, 21–39. Nijmegen

Index